The Female Line

Researching your Female Ancestors

Margaret Ward

COUNTRYSIDE BOOKS
3 Catherine Road
Newbury, Berkshire

To view our complete range of books,
please visit us at
www.countrysidebooks.co.uk

ISBN 1 85306 818 7

For Mum – Diana Margaret Orchin, née Milbourne

The cover photograph shows two branches of the Vulliamy family,
daughters all, together in 1887.

Typeset by Textype, Cambridge
Produced through MRM Associates Ltd., Reading
Printed by J. W. Arrowsmith Ltd., Bristol

Contents

Introduction

Our female ancestors bore the children and raised them, they cared for the old and the sick, they worked both in the home and outside it. They were usually the ones who kept the family together and in touch, who stored away old letters and photographs, who knew what happened to Cousin Flo and Great Aunt Betty and why Uncle Jack never mentioned his first wife. They observed life around them, in the home and town or village and, if we are lucky, they recorded it in diaries and letters, or they handed down the stories orally to their children and grandchildren. This is not to belittle the role played by men in family life; to want to know more about these women is just an acknowledgement that they have far too often been the strong but invisible roots of the family tree.

There comes a time in family history when the accumulation of names, dates and places is not enough any more. We might have the certificates and the parish register entries, the wills and the census returns, and the tree is bushing out nicely in all directions, and yet we may feel we really do not know anything at all about our ancestors – about the lives they led, the choices they had, the limitations that held them back, and the forces that propelled them forward.

This applies particularly to the women, both single and married, in our family trees, who may not have had interesting jobs that we can research, and who stayed at home when the men went off to war. How much, for instance, do you know about the lives of the women in your family at the time of the First World War, when their husbands and fathers were at the front?

This is a book of possibilities – an introduction to putting the spotlight on the female line, taking as a convenience the starting point of 1800 and coming forward in time to the end of the Second World War. It is intended to show what a wide and interesting range of topics can be included as 'women's family history', in the hope that you will want to go on and investigate further by including social and local history in your own research. Such a large proportion of women's lives was lived privately and will not be recorded in historical archives, but wanting to find out about what marriage may have meant to them, or how they were viewed by the law and by society, gives an added dimension to any family tree. There are suggestions here for the kind of questions you can ask to highlight what you want to know – no easy matter when the subject is so vast – and the quest won't be easy, but where would be the enjoyment if it was?

Including the relatively recent Second World War in the timeline for this book means that many readers may have personal experience of some of the topics covered. I have wavered between using the words 'ancestor' and 'relative' in the text, but please see them both simply as shorthand for 'a female member of your family, present or past'! I hope you enjoy beginning to follow your Female Line.

Margaret Ward

CHAPTER 1

Following the Female Line

When W.P.W. Phillimore explained *How to Write the History of a Family* in 1887, he believed it doubtful 'whether any genealogist has ever compiled a pedigree which included female lines only . . . the female lines in England at least are usually disregarded, although some ardent American genealogists endeavour to include all the descendants of a common ancestor . . . But we must remember that, as a rule, genealogists in the United States usually do not trace back their pedigrees for more than a couple of centuries'. Which put them in their place; if you have generations of men to put in your tree, why bother with the women?

Things have changed since 1887, of course, though perhaps not as much as they should have done. The grip of the male line has been tenacious, and it is often the fault, as you are probably well aware, of the identification of the 'family' with the surname it bears.

The name's the problem

'Most people are interested in names,' wrote P.H. Reaney in *The Origin of English Surnames* (1967). It may have been curiosity about their name that brought many people into family history in the first place, and we all of us keep an eye out for our name (in all its variety of spellings) in any list or document that we come across.

The trouble with women is that they change their name, sometimes with depressing frequency. All in all, women are awkward creatures to fit into conventional family trees. An entry in the burial register for Great Amwell records *Elizabeth Wilkinson by birth, Elizabeth Sheafe by marriage, Elizabeth Davis by common forme, Elizabeth Chandler by usual appelation, neyther mayde, wife, nor widdowe, after an unquiete lyfe a languishing sicknesse and a desyred death was buried the nyneth of Julye 1632.*

An unquiet life indeed, but that example will have struck a chord with many a family historian. Tracing women can prove a real problem. They start off with their father's name. Then if they marry they (usually) take their husband's name. And if they separate or divorce, they may go back to their maiden name, or keep the husband's, or remarry and take yet another name. And if you have a marriage certificate that shows your lady is a divorcée or widow, how can you be sure whether the name she has given as her 'previous name' is her maiden name, or her ex-husband's? It could take you on a fruitless quest for the wrong family if you aren't careful.

Some people stoutly protest that they *are* following the female line – they are tracing their mother's family, as well as that of their father. Good for them, but if in fact what they are doing is following their mother's surname, which is, of course, her father's name, there you are, straight back to a male line once again and dependent on a surname.

So how can you redress the balance and make women the central characters in your family tree? And how can you then go on to discover more about those women and the lives they lived?

You may decide to create a tree that shows only your direct female line – your mother, your mother's mother, your grandmother's mother, and so on. This does have one advantage. Without casting aspersions on your ancestors, how do you know that the man whose name you are so diligently researching was in fact the father of the child produced by his wife? They do say that the only ancestor you can be completely sure of is the mother! Brian Sykes, Professor of Human Genetics at Oxford, contends that 90 per cent of modern Europeans are descended from just seven 'matriarchs', one unchanging gene being passed on by a mother to all her children, on down the generations (*The Seven Daughters of Eve*, Corgi, 2002).

Most family historians, however, will probably decide to simply look a little more into the lives of their female ancestors. Do add in the sisters of each generation, married and unmarried. This does give you the advantage of having lots of women to research, with potential for interesting stories. With all those sisters and cousins and aunts, what a wonderful array of female experience over the centuries you will come up with!

The importance of a woman's female relatives in bringing up her children cannot be over-emphasised. After all, it is to her own mother's home that she may return to bear her first child; it is her sisters she gossips with and writes to; it's her mother's style of cooking that she learned and that is passed down to her daughters as well. Men carry the surname; they have an occupation we can find out about; they go to war and they sometimes lead lives of more obvious action and incident. Women may just slip through history, sometimes unseen, insubstantial and forgotten. But you can be sure that when they were living, breathing beings, those women had an influence on the people around them that we are probably still feeling today.

How does this all differ from male-line research? On the whole, not a lot, if you think in terms of the records consulted. Civil registration, the census, wills, parish registers and other papers from the parish chest will still form the backbone of your research. True, there will be a divergence at times – finding out what your grandmother or great-aunt did during the war will take you through different sources, perhaps, from those for tracing a soldier male ancestor. You'll still be looking at the IGI and other main genealogical sources, at newspapers and court reports, at directories, at workhouse and school records, and inscriptions on gravestones. But you may be looking for different names in each generation, and, because society viewed your female ancestor differently from your male ancestor, legally, morally and economically, you too may have to adjust the way you think about your research.

Starting with yourself

Every book on beginning family history tells you to start with what you know and work backwards. This sound advice, which is often ignored in the excitement of wanting to get back as far as possible as quickly as

A contrast of female cycling outfits in 1899 – a telling indication of the new freedoms young women were demanding at the end of the 19th century.

possible, is even more important when you want to gain a perspective on women of the past. (I am now going to assume just for a while that my reader is a woman and I apologise to male family historians reading this section – perhaps you could try out the following ideas with your wife or daughter, sister or girlfriend?)

Before doing anything else, concentrate on yourself for a moment. Recognising the changes that have taken place within your own lifetime – in the home and at work, in behaviour, in law, in society, in leisure – will be a great starting point for moving back through the generations. Yes, you can simply build up a female family tree as usual, adding names and dates as you go, and it will be tremendous fun to do. But wouldn't you like to try to understand the kind of lives your ancestors led, too? We may never be able to truly know what our ancestors thought about or cared about, but we can do our best to put them into perspective and into their own place in history.

So, why not take the time to make a start on your own life story. First set down the bare bones of your own life – birth and baptism dates, education, work, marriage, etc. Then, when you have that framework, start jotting down memories of school, work and life at home. Perhaps old letters, postcards, school reports, family photographs or any of the other bits of family memorabilia we all have tucked away will spark off other trains of thought. Just keep writing. Try, too, to consider the kind of choices you have been able to make in your own life. What kind of education did you have? Are you married, or single and independent? Did you feel pressure to get married as a mark of 'success'? Are you divorced? Do you manage your own money? Do you vote? Do you work outside the home? Did you have a choice about the work you followed?

If you think this is all rather time-wasting and nothing to do with family history, please think again. This is what history is all about – the flow of change that we all experience. By starting with ourselves, we get a touchstone for change and as we go back through the years it will be a huge help in understanding the context within which our ancestors lived. Because now you've thought about yourself, do the same thing for your mother. And then, as much as you are able, for your grandmother. Interesting, isn't it?

Don't ignore or disparage the domestic side of life. For many women, memories about their home and families will be every bit as important as those about work or great events. Don't you think it was just the same for your ancestors? In fact, researching domestic life is fascinating. How did your grandmother cook food in a cottage without an oven? Where did she get her water from? How *did* she fit a family of twelve into a two up, two down cottage? A good introduction to the subject is *A Woman's Work is Never Done: a History of Housework in the British Isles 1650–1900* by Caroline Davidson (Chatto & Windus, 1986).

When you've finished, don't throw your jottings away. Why not use them as the launchpad for your autobiography? Wouldn't you love to have something similar written by your great-grandmother?

If there was something going on in the village, these two would know about it. You may discover a great deal about the family and local life from female relatives.

Talk to your older female relatives

If you have not already done so, now is the time to talk to all your elderly female relatives. Draw up a list of them and don't wait until it is too late – we've all got stories of how we *were* going to get in touch but time went by and Great-aunt Rose died and with her went forever all the family stories and memories.

Women, on the whole, have a greater curiosity about what is going on around them in the family and the community than men do. The Reverend Sydney Smith, Rector of Wombwell, recalled in his *Reminiscences of a Sheffield Ministry* (1926) one day as a young curate taking the mothers' meeting excursion to Stony Middleton. Having left the ladies to eat their picnic lunch, the curate and his vicar then returned to take them on a tour of 'the beauties of the neighbourhood'. The ladies could not be found. After an exhaustive search of the village, they were discovered in the churchyard, 'sitting upon the gravestones, waiting for a funeral procession to emerge from the church'. The vicar and curate could not understand this morbid interest in someone the ladies had never met and knew nothing about: 'We came to the conclusion that doubtless they would discuss the "widow" and wonder how "he" had treated her and what "he" had left her. They would further surmise as to the relationship of each of the mourners to the "corpse". They would, too, discuss the dress and funeral accoutrement of the various mourners as the procession passed along and so altogether they would extract for themselves, one supposes, a certain amount of incident and sightseeing which all helped to make up a "happy day".'

I have seen it written somewhere that 'old men forget, old women remember'. Your older female relatives will be able to tell you so much that you would otherwise never know, including tales of people you never knew and who apparently bear no relation to you whatsoever. Write them all down! You don't know when something will suddenly make sense and produce a connection you never suspected. Separating the truth from the gossip may sometimes present a problem, but don't dismiss apparently outlandish stories until you have tested them with your own research. Equally, don't accept everything you are told at face value!

If you have never approached relatives before, and especially if they are comparative strangers to you, you need to give some thought to it beforehand. Some people will take you to their hearts immediately and you will get on wonderfully, with never an awkward moment; others won't. You should have a clear idea of what information you want – names and dates and so on. Take photographs, and a family tree of what you know so far; visual aids like these are a great help in jogging memories and helping to clarify whose cousin or sister you are talking about. But you also want to go beyond the strictly genealogical (and this may take more than one visit). You will have ideas from the autobiographical notes you made earlier and from the following chapters. Use those to start to flesh out the lives of the female members of your family tree.

You are there to discover what it was like being a woman in her generation and what happened to her grandmother, her mother and sisters and aunts and cousins. You might, if you get a good relationship going, even be able to persuade her to write her own memoirs. You might, if you are very lucky, find a great friend across the generations.

The Jenkins family at Christmas 1903. Disentangling family relationships can be a problem, even when you have the 'evidence' in front of you. Don't delay in asking older relatives if they recognise people in family photographs.

CHAPTER 2

What Did She Look Like?

What did she look like? This is one of the most intriguing questions we can ask about our female ancestors. The sad fact is that, more often than not, we are unlikely to be able to supply an answer. But that shouldn't stop us trying, and, apart from those of our relatives we know personally or those who can be described for us by someone who did know them, it is going to be to photographs that we turn first for an answer.

Family photographs

It was in the 1840s, with the opening of the first professional photographic studio in London by Richard Beard, that the importance of the photograph for family history began. By the 1850s, advances in technology had lowered prices and created a market for portraits amongst all classes. Demand soared: in 1851 only 51 commercial photographers were recorded in the census, but by 1861 this figure had risen to over 2,500. Photographs could soon be taken not only on commercial premises but also in fairground booths and on the streets, so that it would only have been the poorest of families who could not afford to pay for a photograph to mark a special occasion or a day out.

Not all of those early photographers were men. In recent years there has been new interest in the handful of early female pioneers, such as Julia Margaret Cameron (1815–79), or Ada Constance Terson

A memento of a day out? These ladies are standing on grass, and the photographic mount is blank – perhaps the work of a travelling photographer? Those pronounced leg-of-mutton sleeves were fashionable in the later 1890s.

(1862–1925), a collection of whose work is held at Dover Museum. Dover can also claim one of the first professional women photographers to have had her own high street studio in the 1920s: Dorothy Sherwood. It should also be remembered that many male photographers were assisted by their wives, whose expertise was sadly never acknowledged.

In the 1880s George Eastman designed the first Kodak camera and in 1900 the famous box Brownie camera went on sale. Taking 'snapshots' was to become an enormously popular hobby. The old studio photographs did not disappear from the family album, but from the early 1900s you may be able to find more relaxed and casual shots of your family than had been possible before. Women, in particular, took to this new hobby with great enthusiasm, and much of the advertising for new cameras and for film was aimed at them. *The Story of Popular Photography* (ed. Colin Ford, National Museum of Photography, Film & Television, 1989) quotes 'a Birmingham newspaper' in 1905: 'Thousands of Birmingham girls are scattered about the holiday resorts of Britain . . . and a very large percentage of them are armed with cameras, mainly, of course, of the hand variety.' Perhaps you can thank the women in your family for most of those irreplaceable snapshots in your album.

Ask every relative you know of, whether they hold any photographs of older members of the family. Don't delay this; do it now. Photographs are precious and extremely vulnerable, but these days it is simple to make copies, whether photographic, computer-scanned or photocopied, though you will naturally want the very best copy you can afford. Don't forget to build up a library of current women family members too. And make sure that every photograph you have is clearly marked with the name(s) of the people shown, who they are (i.e. where in the family tree they belong), where they are, and the date. We all think we are going to be able to remember such details, but we don't, and if you get knocked down by a bus tomorrow the secrets will go with you. That is why it is also important to sit down with members of the family and go through old albums, making notes of *who* and *where* and *when* as you go.

You could also make enquiries to find out whether family photo-

Sometimes not every photograph in an album is of a member of the family. This benign old lady turned out to be a popular actress called Mrs Stirling, whose career spanned 1833 to 1886. Many people collected photographs of actresses or royalty and included them in their family album.

graphs have been diverted down another branch of the family tree. Your mother may have no photographs of her mother's family, but that is not to say that her aunt or a cousin did not claim the family album when the older generation died. It would not be unusual for a family branch with a different name from your own and perhaps very little interest in the subject to have something precious to you in their possession. Not that you have any right to lay claim to the album, of course – but a polite enquiry may yield riches and friendly persuasion should lead to your being allowed to have some of the photographs copied.

Outside the family

Supposing you have no family photographs at all, even after ransacking the attic and approaching all your known relatives? Perhaps you could try working around the problem from a different direction, and look for your family photos in public places.

Photographs started appearing in local newspapers, for instance, from the turn of the century, and by the 1920s and 1930s editors were taking full advantage of the selling power of having your picture in the paper. Weddings, unusual achievements or anniversaries, workplace celebrations, sporting events: all, and more, could feature someone in your family. Of course, if they achieved notoriety for some reason, national newspapers will also be a source.

The last few years have seen the publication of a huge number of books of old photographs. Check them all for your area (and, since few seem to have indexes, you have to read the captions carefully). Many of the people pictured will be unnamed, but some books produced by local people can be mines of information. Don't forget, too, that books produced to celebrate the anniversaries of particular firms, and trade journals, may have photographs of the workers.

Record offices, museums, local studies libraries and reference libraries will usually have collections of old photographs, sometimes comprehensively catalogued, sometimes not. Your ancestor could appear as a named individual, or as part of a group. School class photos, sometimes to be found with other school records in record offices, are useful, and doubly so if someone has taken the trouble to write down the names of the children. Local history societies may also be worth approaching; one I know of has a collection of village wedding photographs.

Other ways to picture her

If photographs elude you, or you are researching an ancestor dating from a time before photography was a possibility, by what other means could you recreate a physical presence for your ancestor?

What about written descriptions? Female criminals, for instance, may be described in official records or in newspaper reports either as they pass through the justice system or if they are being searched for by the police. They may not always be attractive descriptions, but they are at least honest. Mary Ann Fallon was under suspicion of theft from her employers in 1837: 'She is about forty years of age, middle stature, pitted with the smallpox, leans her head on one side, and is deaf; dressed in a dirty striped cotton gown, black bonnet, and old boots.' (*Police Gazette*, 'Hue and Cry', 5 April 1837)

If your ancestor had to wear a uniform at any point in her life, you can at least find out what she would have looked like in that! People in uniform often look very similar to each other, and there is no shame in having to say that 'Great-grandmother wore a uniform like this' rather than producing an actual likeness of her. It would also be the case that women living in, perhaps, a fishing village on the east coast of Yorkshire would all have had a certain similarity about their appearance, at least regarding clothing – depictions of a locality may be the best you can hope for. Countrywomen probably retained older-fashioned garments for longer than their urban counterparts. When money was short, fashion efforts might manifest themselves in new trimmings, or a new hair ribbon, or new hat, rather than a complete new outfit. A cape or shawl, a hard-wearing skirt and an apron constituted a uniform in itself, which lasted throughout the 19th century and was only superseded in the 20th century by the housecoat or 'pinnie' and cardigan.

And lastly, it may seem a long shot, but have you considered that your ancestors may have had their portraits painted? If they were

The hat worn by the sitter and the 'head and shoulders' vignette, suggest the 1880s/1890s. The back of the carte gives exact addresses for the studios of T. Smith & Sons and it should be fairly simple to use trade directories to find out when they were in business at those places.

wealthy or locally prominent, it is certainly a possibility, and sometimes if they were neither. Until her death in the 1950s, my great-aunt Jane Wallis worked for many years in Kensington as a housekeeper for an artist, Ruth Lacon-Watson, and her husband. I am lucky enough to have an oil painting of my great-grandfather and a watercolour sketch of another great-aunt, done by Mrs Lacon-Watson from snapshots. If you have a family connection, however remote, with an artist, you might find that they used a relative of yours as a model.

Few cabinet prints were as relaxed, if not provocative, as this portrait of an unknown young woman, probably dating to the 1880s.

Finding out more

You have photographs and you're fairly sure who the subject is, but you're not quite sure of the date? Or perhaps you need a rough date to be able to make a guess as to who the woman in the photograph is? Robert Pols has written several books on dating and identifying old photographs, including *Dating Old Photographs* (Federation of Family History Societies, 2nd edition 1998), *Looking at Old Photographs: their Dating and Interpretation* (FFHS, 1999) and *Family Photographs 1860-1945* (PRO, 2002). The magazine *Practical Family History* runs a series called 'Shots in the Dark' whereby readers send in unidentified photographs in the hope other readers may be able to help.

To make the most of your detective work into old photographs, you will want to discover how to date them from an analysis of what the women shown in them are wearing. Understanding the complexities of women's fashions can be a little daunting, but the more you read, look constructively at photographs and other pictures, and investigate the social and historical background of fashion, the clearer and more interesting it becomes. Books on fashion and everyday clothing abound and are usually well illustrated. Avril Lansdell's *Fashion à la Carte 1860–1900* (Shire, 1985) is a useful guide to dating cartes de visite from the clothing of the sitters; *Everyday Dress 1650–1900* by Elizabeth Ewing (Batsford, 1984) is a very readable history of fashion and much more. For more unusual clothing, two books by Phillis Cunnington and Catherine Lucas may be helpful: *Occupational Costume in England* (A. & C. Black, 1968) and *Charity Costumes* (A. & C. Black, 1978). On the Internet, the website *www.fashion-era.com* has a colourful chronology of Victorian and 20th century clothing and a bibliography of useful sources and places to visit, such as the Museum of Costume at Bath (Assembly Rooms, Bennett Street).

3

Merry Wives? Marriage, Women and the Law

'Women's mission on earth is of course to inspire love, with the ultimate object of getting married,' declared Augustus Mayhew, slightly tongue-in-cheek, in *Faces for Fortunes* (1867). Nineteenth-century writers (and some later ones too) tended to see marriage as the end of a woman's story – mission achieved. Family historians, on the other hand, might like to look on marriage as the start of another story, a sea change in a woman's life, sometimes for the better, sometimes for the worse.

How did she meet him?

Have you ever wondered how your ancestors met their husbands-to-be? If she came from Manchester and he came from Truro and they married in London in 1851, how on earth did they happen to meet, let alone get to know each other and plan to spend the rest of their lives together? Or if they came from the same parish, how exactly did they first approach each other?

A middle class girl was unlikely to marry outside her class throughout the 19th century and well into the 20th century. Her mother and other older female relatives would control quite strictly the type of men she met and mixed with. Father's permission might be needed for the young man to gain his daughter's hand in marriage, but his pre-occupation could very well be with finances and prospects, while Mother's assessment of whether the suitor was 'the right type' or 'one of us' would be crucial. Daughter would be chaperoned at all times, and rarely allowed out alone.

Working class girls, on the other hand, might or might not stay strictly within class boundaries. The number of women marrying 'upwards', into the lower middle class world of blue collar workers and shopkeepers, seems to have increased over the 19th century. Domestic service could easily fit a girl for something better: the lessons learned – both of how to run a household and of a life beyond the parish boundary – would not be lost on an intelligent and ambitious girl, who might very well come to want something better for her own life than what her mother had experienced. 'Butchers and milkmen were favoured as husbands,' wrote Flora Thompson in *Lark Rise to Candleford* of country girls who had gone into service in the 1880s; callers at the door were watched closely in many households in case the servants got romantic ideas and encouraged 'followers'.

It had traditionally been the case that the daughter of a man in the skilled artisan trades would look for a husband among the sons of similar workers. Shoemakers' daughters frequently married shoe-makers' sons, for instance, and you may very well find this kind of pattern in your own family. These were in essence workplace marriages. As factories took over from the old home-based industries, more marriages would emerge from the factory floor and the office. We still most frequently find our partners at work. Religious or immigrant groups would have their own influence on marriage. Quakers and Jews were subject to strict embargos over marriage choices; until 1860 any Quaker girl who married outside the sect would be disowned and evicted from the Society of Friends. The trauma of losing contact with friends and family should not be underestimated. Other nonconformist sects also had strong trading and social links which bound them together. Immigrants would naturally stick together, creating little Russias, Italys, and so on within the cities.

People's horizons were surprisingly restricted, whatever their origins, and if your ancestor lived in a large town or city it does not

No laughing matter for many women left holding the baby. Her options were limited – find another man, or lose either the baby or her job.

necessarily mean that they looked too far outward from their home or workplace. 'A family which moves two miles away is completely lost to view . . . Even relatives cease to be actively interested in their fate', noted Maud Pember-Reeves of the families living in Lambeth in the early 1900s (*Round about a Pound a Week*, 1913). Workplace, neighbourhood, family get-togethers, church or chapel – the meeting places that brought couples together in the 19th century were not so varied as they could be by the 1930s, and these rather prosaic alternatives may have been the route to romance for most young couples.

Many a girl, however, fell for the lure of a uniform or a handsome stranger. Did your ancestor marry a soldier or militiaman, who was perhaps on manoeuvres in the countryside far from his home town? Or could they have met at the local market town when the annual fair was in full swing? Was her beloved a stonemason or carpenter who had come to her neighbourhood to help rebuild the parish church? Or perhaps they were in service together at some large house, or he was a travelling man, a drover maybe, who wooed and won a girl from a village he passed through on his regular route? It is interesting to speculate about the forces that could have brought two people together.

Meeting, however, was one thing; actually getting married was another. Marriage was not likely to be on the cards for a couple until there was a possibility of their having their own home, or at least a room to themselves, so engagements (or betrothals) might last a long time. A long engagement might also be encouraged by the couple's parents. For some families, the money earned by an older child could make all the difference in the continuing struggle against poverty.

Flora Thompson describes how, as soon as a cottage in Lark Rise became vacant, word would be sent to the betrothed girl at her workplace and she would immediately give notice and come home to the village to marry. By the end of the 19th century, however, there was a serious shortfall of houses available for rent in urban areas (only the wealthy would have bought a house in those days) and many a girl faced either a long wait or the prospect of starting married life sharing a home – in big cities, of course, the majority of residents may have had to share accommodation, living in just one or two rooms. Council-house building, particularly at the end of the First World War, when the government promised 'homes fit for heroes', did provide some couples with their first home. Both my grandmothers started married life in newly-built council houses in Chelmsford, Essex.

If you get on well with your older female relatives, it would be interesting to find out what local courting customs were – if they'll tell you. Unfortunately, many older women will clam up completely on the subject, or insist that everyone was a lot more moral in *their* day. That's their prerogative; so this is only a subject for those you get on *very well* with! You may find out more from oral history projects in your locality, and there have been many autobiographies of 'ordinary' women published in the last few years which offer a wealth of information.

Privacy was a luxury few could afford and if your ancestors were working class they probably conducted their courting in a privately public manner. In *The Classic Slum*, Robert Roberts describes couples in Salford in the early 1900s walking the streets together and cuddling in doorways – as private a place as they could find. Country girls could meet their sweethearts in the fields, away from prying eyes, though everyone would know where they had gone: 'whispering and kissing and making love until the dusk deepened and it was time for the girl to go home, for no respectable girl was supposed to be out after ten' (*Lark Rise to Candleford*).

And was your ancestor a respectable girl? No question is too personal for a family historian to ask, though you may not get an answer! You may well find instances in your family tree of brides who must have been pregnant when they wed, with the baptism of the first child recorded as less than nine months from the wedding date. Sometimes considerably less. It seems that in the first half of the 19th century, about one-third of first children were born within eight months of marriage. It was a 'custom' in some areas (particularly where children were valued for their earning capacity) for marriage only to take place when a woman was pregnant, the idea being that she had thus proved her fertility.

As a very general rule, and despite what your great-aunt may say, it seems that pre-marital sex was not frowned on as long as the couple concerned were betrothed and did get married in the end. 'It was accounted no shame for a child to be begotten out of wedlock – the shame was when there was no wedding to follow. That was something almost unknown – something that didn't stand thinking about,' recalled Margaret Penn, who was born in 1900 near Manchester (quoted in *Destiny Obscure*, see below).

A betrothal was taken as seriously as any other contract, although nothing was required in writing to make it mutually binding. Breaking that agreement might have terrible consequences for the woman involved: she could be seen as 'unfit' for marriage; she would certainly suffer gossip and innuendo; and she might even be left pregnant with no prospect of putting the situation right in the eyes of her family and friends. If the man broke the engagement at the last minute, the bride's family had probably expended a substantial amount of money, as it was (and frequently still is) the bride's father who paid for the wedding celebration. A suit in the courts for breach of promise was no easy option, requiring the girl to stand up in public and give evidence against her former lover, but it might be resorted to – and not only by the wealthier sections of society. At Hertford Assizes in 1852, for instance, Emma Oldaker, a republican's daughter, brought an action against George Davis, a farmer; the jury decided for the defendant. On the other hand, in 1890, Miss Gladys Knowles took Mr Leslie Duncan, editor of *Matrimonial News*, before the assizes at Lewes, and the details of her attempted seduction, reported fully in *The Times* (13 August 1890), gained her £10,000 in damages, a huge amount of money at the time. A sad, pretty young lady could exact serious financial revenge for her humiliation!

The wedding

Apart from the actual marriage certificate (from 1837; before that, the entry in the parish register), what can help you to get a little closer to your ancestor on her wedding day? You may have already discovered letters, invitation cards, even an engraved gift that has survived the years. Talking to older female relatives may uncover other mementoes. There could even be a wedding dress folded away in a trunk somewhere!

The best discovery, though, from the late 19th century onward, would be the wedding photograph. Most families have photos tucked away somewhere – groups of stiffly dressed men and women carefully arranged, perhaps in the back garden or somewhere equally incongruous. The women's hats always seem particularly significant! The joy of these photographs is that, if you have several dating from different periods, you can follow the changes in fashion through the years, from the Victorians right through to the wartime brides of the 1940s. And, if they are a family without too much money, you can be sure that the bridegroom was still wearing his wedding suit for best for many years after that photograph was taken.

If the woman you are interested in came from a middle class family, or from a family well known in their own locality, there may be a report of the wedding in the local newspaper. If there is, you are indeed lucky, for these can go on for several paragraphs, listing not only who was there and what relationship they were to the bride and groom, but all the wedding presents and what the principals were wearing to boot. Take this excerpt from a long newspaper report in the *Hertfordshire Mercury*, 12 April 1929, of the marriage of Miss Dora Mary Rhoda Warboys:

> The bride, who was given away by her father, was attired in white satin, in Italian medieval style, with Medici collar of Italian needle lace, and veil of the same material. Her only jewellery was a triple row of pearls, and she carried a sheaf of Easter lilies. She was attended by four bridesmaids, the Misses Marjorie and Dorothy Rowland, Miss Molly Bowden (cousins), and Miss Nellie Rowland (aunt) and another cousin Master James Rowland, acted as page. The maids were dressed in orchid mauve chiffon, with floral coats to tone, large tulle picture hats of the same colour, and they carried bouquets of mauve and blue sweet peas, and wore necklaces of pearls. The little page was dressed in orchid mauve satin in Kate Greenaway style.

Poor little page boy! But what a feast for a family historian.

Sometimes there is a clue in the photograph that this was a couple's wedding picture: although the young woman's right hand is gloved, her left hand, displaying two fine rings, is prominently displayed. Unfortunately, their photographer clumsily left in shot the metal brace that is keeping her head at the right angle!

A contemporary postcard making quite sure that young Edwardian women understood that politics and romance could not mix. (Terry Pankhurst Collection)

In the eyes of the law

In the early 1800s, as soon as she said 'I do' and signed the wedding register, your ancestor lost not only her surname, but also her identity, and in the eyes of the law she became almost a non-person. All her property automatically became the property of her husband.

An exception might be any land, property, shares, etc. that was protected by a marriage settlement, perhaps drawn up by her protective father, or personal items that were lumped together as her 'paraphernalia'. Such settlements were often made as a matter of course in middle class marriages, ensuring some financial independence and protection for the woman against a spendthrift, or even downright mercenary, husband. In general, though, a married woman owned nothing – not the clothes she stood up in, not the cash in her purse, not a stick of furniture, not a piece of jewellery. Marriage was a very serious business for a woman.

In 1870 the Married Women's Property Act allowed women to keep as their own any wages or earnings they might acquire after that date. It said nothing, however, about the property or money they had been in possession of before marrying. This was rectified by a follow-up act in 1882. From this point, a married woman could own her own 'separate property' and she could hold it or dispose of it as she wished, by will or by any other means. She could also run a business or carry on a trade in her own right, and she would be liable for her own contracts and debts.

It follows that more married women left wills from the 1870s onwards. However, wills or letters of administration relating to the property of married women are by no means unknown before that date and are well worth checking the will registers for. Working out how your married ancestor came to leave a will could be interesting – was her family better off than her husband's? Was there a marriage settlement? Was she perhaps legally separated from her husband and therefore, after 1857, entitled to possession of her own earnings?

Separation and divorce

You may already know that your ancestor was separated or divorced, perhaps from family stories, or you may simply suspect that something is not quite right, as you trace her movement from place to place and find the once married couple always living apart at census time. A new family may even appear in the records, with no corresponding trace of the death of the first spouse.

At the beginning of the 19th century there were few options open for a woman who wanted to leave her husband, whether she was rich or poor. Any marriage dispute was still the province of the ecclesiastical courts, as it had been for centuries. Unless there were grounds for proclaiming a marriage null and void (if, for instance, the couple were within the prohibited degrees of kinship, or one of them was unable to consummate the marriage), in the eyes of the Church no marriage legally entered into could be declared ended for any reason; it followed that remarriage, too, could never be an option.

The very wealthy or well-connected might solve the problem by obtaining a divorce by a private Act of Parliament. First resorted to in the 17th century, few followed this route until the 18th century. There were 74 private divorce acts in the last quarter of that century and another 90 in the next 50 years – still small numbers, but an indication that demand was growing. Only four women, though, ever managed to initiate a divorce in this way.

So what could a woman do if she found herself trapped in marriage with an abusive, adulterous, or cruel partner? Or if she simply fell in love with someone else? Very little, I'm afraid. A man had 'law, power and dominion' over his wife. Men believed, and the law backed them up in this on many occasions, that they had the right to chastise their wives. In other words, they could beat them if 'provoked'. The old rhyme, 'A woman, a dog and a walnut tree, the more you beat them the better they be', would have described practice acceptable to a great many men. In a series of court decisions, it became customary to agree that it was all right to beat your wife as long as you used a stick no bigger than a man's thumb in width! Only if the man used a little too much force, would the law step in.

One option for a battered wife was to apply to the local magistrates for 'security of the peace'. A violent husband would be required to stand surety that he would not continue to ill-treat her. However, she still had to live with him after the case was over, and would have had to go back to court if the situation deteriorated once more (although in cases of serious assault, concerned magistrates occasionally agreed to a legal separation). In 1828 common assault and battery (and not just towards women) became a summary offence, to be tried before one or two magistrates sitting without a jury – a much quicker system. However, to take out a criminal prosecution against her husband, a woman would have to pay the legal bill, which put even this flimsy protection beyond the reach of the majority of women. A married woman, after all, did not usually have any money of her own.

Details of cases brought by wives against their husbands can be found, in local quarter or petty sessions records, and they were often

Women in a Salvation Army shelter in Whitechapel in 1892 (from The Graphic*). Leaving a marriage and coping on your own was not a decision to be taken lightly when destitution might be the result.*

reported in local newspapers. Later in the century, for example, the *Woodbridge Reporter* (June 1875) noted that William Broom of Clopton, Suffolk was before the courts for having threatened to kill his wife, Ellen: 'she called him to find sureties to keep the peace towards her . . . The court took his own recognisance for six months and he was discharged.' He was back before the court for assaulting her in August, and no doubt poor Ellen suffered much more from him in the course of their marriage.

In the early 19th century, if she wanted to leave a brutish husband entirely, there was not much a woman could do except disappear one day and never come back. But then he could go to the ecclesiastical court to demand restitution of his conjugal rights, and there would be no protection for her if he took her back by force. If her husband agreed, they might draw up a private separation agreement between themselves (which the court would not recognise), but this did not waive the husband's legal right to custody of his wife and he could always get her back if he wanted to.

She could try to petition the ecclesiastical court for a separation *a mensa et thoro* ('from bed and board') on grounds of cruelty. If successful, she could live safely apart from her husband, who would have to pay her alimony, but the separation did not allow her to marry again and in the eyes of the law she remained 'a wife'. She might also face some difficulty in proving that the cruelty was such as to justify separation – violence had to be physical and to have left its mark. At the beginning of the 19th century, this strict application was just beginning to be relaxed to sometimes take into account the actual threat of violence.

Left with no alternative, the poor might remarry bigamously (which was of course illegal), live together 'in sin', or occasionally indulge in 'wife-selling', which was still being reported as late as the 1850s. The latter term seems to suggest a cruel act imposed upon women by their husbands, but in practice it seems to have been an effective mechanism for a woman who wanted to leave her husband to set up home with another man. For instance, the *Hampshire Courier* reported on 31 October 1814: that 'A labouring man, of Westham, led his wife, a decently-dressed woman, into the market in a halter, and there exhibited her for sale, in which situation, however, he had not long placed her, before a tradesman of a neighbouring parish stepped up and bargained for her at five shillings! She was accordingly delivered, and her purchaser ... took her off in triumph, amid the congratulations of a great number of spectators.' (Quoted in *News from the English Countryside 1750–1850* by Clifford Morsley, Harrap, 1979.) The key seems to be the public nature of these 'sales', and the affability of all concerned. Bigamy was a capital crime until 1861, when punishment was lightened to seven years' transportation or two years' imprisonment.

Divorce – the legal termination of a marriage – was never recognised by the ecclesiastical courts. After a long campaign by its supporters, the Matrimonial Causes Act was passed in 1857, coming into force on 1 January 1858. Responsibility for hearing cases of matrimonial separation was taken away from the ecclesiastical courts and given to the newly created divorce court (properly the Court for Divorce and Matrimonial Causes, part of the Probate, Divorce and Admiralty Division of the Supreme Court). However, as there was only one divorce court, and that was in London, it was still only wealthier women who could afford to pursue a legal fight to end their marriage. Women could now apply for a divorce on the grounds of a husband's adultery, but it had to be aggravated by incest, bigamy, rape, sodomy, bestiality, cruelty or desertion. A man, on the other hand, could divorce his wife for adultery alone. The obvious injustice of this continued to be a bone of contention with women's rights reformers through the remainder of the century and it was not addressed by the law until 1923. It was also not until the 1920s that divorce cases could be heard locally, in a number of assize towns around the country.

Because a divorce act was now on the books (several times revised over the next century), it would be wrong to forget that divorce itself remained socially unacceptable and that most women would simply put up with a bad marriage rather than approach the courts. The number of divorce suits was however steadily rising by the 1930s and the enforced separation of the Second World War produced even more. Amanda Bevan ('Divorce 1858 onwards': *Ancestors*, October/November 2002) quotes the case of one assize town where 320 divorce suits were dealt with in six and a half days in 1946!

A witness being cross-examined in the Divorce Court (from George Sims' Living London*). Divorce proceedings always provoked interest and will usually be reported in the local newspaper (and the nationals if the details are scandalous enough).*

Finding out more

Local histories may give details of local population movement at different periods, or when new industries started up or old ones expanded and drew in extra workers, or describe nearby canals or trade routes, all of which might help to explain how strangers met. Look at the wider **community** around where your ancestor lived too: what kind of people would she have encountered every day? Was her family in a business or trade that tended to stick together? This is a good reason for looking at **census** returns and trade **directories** for your area in some detail and not relying on indexes. War is a great impetus to marriage and moves people from their home areas. Don't forget **family legend**, too. So often, Granny's stories of how Great-grandma met Great-grandpa become part of family lore – and quite often we dismiss them as of no significance, just another anecdote. Not now!

Colin Chapman's *Marriage Laws, Rites, Records and Customs* (Lochin

Publishing, 1997) is an excellent source book for all manner of marriage-related subjects, going back to the 16th century; see too *For Better, For Worse, British Marriages 1600 to the Present* by John R. Gillis (OUP, 1985). Colin Chapman has also written *Ecclesiastical Courts; their Officials and their Records* (Lochin Publishing, 1992), which will be helpful if you want to look at the cases relating to marriage brought before the church courts. *Wives and Property* by Lee Holcombe (University of Toronto Press, 1983) recounts the struggle to reform the property laws in the 19th century; and *Road to Divorce: England 1530–1987* by Lawrence Stone is an interesting account of the history of divorce and separation. **Divorce** records are held in the National Archives (Public Record Office). Do read Amanda Bevan's article on 'Divorce 1858 onwards' in the October/November 2002 issue of *Ancestors* magazine, which describes the sometimes complicated records and how to consult them. **Newspapers** probably reported on the more 'interesting' cases. Women's **wills** may give an insight into the way they controlled their money.

Look out for biographical and autobiographical accounts which illuminate the lives of ordinary people, such as those contained in *Destiny Obscure*, edited by John Barnett (Allen Lane, 1982), which go back as far as the 1820s. *Lark Rise to Candleford* by Flora Thompson (Penguin, 2000) is a wonderful description of life in an Oxfordshire village in the late 1800s, while *Round About a Pound a Week* by Maud Pember Reeves (1913; Virago Press, 1999) is a fascinating account of visits made to women living in Lambeth. You will enjoy reading both these books, even if none of your ancestors came from those places!

Books on particular occupations or groups of people also sometimes have interesting insights into marriage matters. Frank Victor Dawes' *Not in Front of the Servants* (Random Century, 1989), for instance, describes the difficulties of having 'followers' and finding time and space for romance below stairs. *Costume for Births, Marriages and Deaths*, by Phillis Cunnington and Catherine Lucas (A & C Black, 1972) is wonderful for dipping into; and there is an excellent book on *Wedding Fashions 1860–1970* by Avril Lansdell (Shire Publications, 1983). You may feel qualified to write something similar on family wedding fashions by the time you're finished!

4

Relicts and Old Virgins

'A little widow is a dangerous thing! She is experienced, accessible, and free, and withal fatally fascinating,' enthused a book on *The Etiquette of Engagement and Marriage*, published in 1903. Widows seemed to attract suspicion (from other women), fascination (from men) and pity (from everyone) in about equal quantities, depending on their age, financial prospects and number of children. Spinsters, on the other hand, simply attracted pity mixed with a little contempt: 'Poor Louisa! She is an old maid. The full grape has shrunk into the withered raisin – just as sweet but not so tempting.' Poor Louisa, described by Augustus Mayhew in 1867, was in her forties and therefore a confirmed spinster. Widows and spinsters can be the forgotten women of family history, which is a great pity since these women were often the backbone of family life.

Widows

You may have come across a gravestone marking the last resting place of, for example 'Jemima Jones, relict of Mr John Jones'. The word *relict* comes via Old French *relicte* from late Latin *relicta*, from *relinquere* 'to leave behind'. It always seems too close a word to 'relic' for comfort. Sometimes, in a kind of belt-and-braces way, Jemima may be called 'widow and relict'. The inference is plain – once Mr Jones had died, Mrs Jones existed merely as something he had left behind, like a piece of discarded luggage.

Women could, of course, be widows for much of their adult lives, and sometimes for a far longer period than they were married. Women do tend to live longer than men, so that it seems likely you will have a high proportion of widows in your family tree over the centuries. It is easy to overlook a widow in the haste to fill in more generations, but do at least follow her life to its end and give some thought to the difficulties – and perhaps pleasures – she may have experienced over the whole of her life.

What kind of life did she have? Was she already an elderly woman, left alone to cope with the inevitable problems of old age? Or was she relatively young, with a family still to bring up and a home to keep for many decades yet? It goes without saying that wealth and class would have a significant effect on what she could expect.

A widow with a little wealth might indeed be a good catch for someone, though she might prefer to enjoy her independence instead. The outlook was less attractive for the poor. There were no old age pensions until 1909 (at age 70), and before that a working class widow would either have had to continue to work for as long as she was able, rely on her children, or seek assistance from the poor law authorities or charities. Poor women had one advantage over their male counterparts – they could continue to work into old age at jobs such as domestic service, laundrywork, cooking, nursing or childcare, or, in areas that had a thriving craft industry, could plait straw or make lace, for example. They might be more welcome in the household of a son or daughter, too, as they could be expected to help out with domestic work and looking after the children.

Perhaps she was lucky enough to qualify for entry to a local almshouse? Often it was stipulated by the benefactor that residence should be offered to poor widows of the village or parish. Under the Old Poor Law, before 1834, she might have received a small 'pension' from the overseers which would enable her to remain in her home and eke out a living in her declining years. After 1834, however, while that might still have been the case in some more enlightened areas, it became more likely that without means of support within the parish, she would have to enter the union workhouse. When state pensions took some of the worry out of old age, it tended to be only the very aged who went into the workhouse.

Charlotte Coleman (aged 94) and Rebecca White (97), the oldest inmates of the Workhouse Infirmary at Wincanton in 1907, as reported in the Sunday Strand.

A younger woman with children to raise would have had to find employment that would pay for the family to survive. Make no mistake, losing her husband was a tragedy not only from a personal point of view but also from an economic one. If the family lived in a tied cottage on an estate, she might lose her home almost immediately. If she could not cope, the workhouse loomed for them all. My great grandmother Mary Ann Asker lost her husband when they were both in their early thirties, in 1881, leaving her with three young children to bring up on her own. Perhaps it is no wonder that my father remembers her as a severe old lady dressed in unrelieved black. You had to be tough to survive.

Old ladies dressed in black seem to have been fairly common right up to the Second World War. Mourning dress was very strictly adhered to in Victorian times, and those who grew up then would have known the rules. Respectability demanded that when there was a death in the family deep mourning would be donned. Some firms made mourning their business, and even the poor would endeavour to find enough money for a bit of black crepe to make bonnets or dresses respectable and respectful. The middle class widow would very gradually work her way through a strictly laid down gradation of mourning. If she remarried at some point, she would be expected to wear grey (*never* white!), and for the marriage itself 'an air of somewhat chastened joy is considered suitable'.

Would the young working class widow remarry? Only if she could find herself a man willing to take on someone else's children, perhaps. None of the widows in my own tree remarried, although every man who was widowed did so. This may say something about the imbalance in numbers between men and women – women always outnumbered men during the 19th century, and the toll of the First World War made matters worse – or simply something about the attractiveness of my female ancestors! What happened in your family?

Single women

'Old maid' and similar unappealing descriptions do for spinsters what 'relict' does for widows, relegating them to unwanted, 'on the shelf', barren twigs on the family tree.

But this was far from the true picture. Many spinster daughters cared for elderly parents or young nieces and nephews, ran the home and the family, had work or careers of their own, were at the forefront of charitable works or put their considerable energies into political and social reform. They deserve to be given their due in our family history researches, even if they did not provide another generation and are marked on the tree with a short line denoting 'no issue'.

The title of this chapter, by the way, comes from a parish register entry for Durham Cathedral, noted by John Titford in *Family Tree Magazine* (December 1999) – 'Mrs Dongworth, Old Virgin, buried 17th June 1779'. Note that she was 'Mrs', not 'Miss'. Presuming that she was indeed single and not just the victim of an unfulfilled marriage, she is a good example of the problems that can arise when tracing single women – when of mature years they may very well be called by such courtesy titles as 'Mrs', or 'Goody' (short for 'Goodwife'), or 'Granny'. It may even go with the job, such as for cooks in domestic service.

How much of a courtesy this actually was is open to doubt if the following story is any indication. It comes from the Revd Smith, who was Chaplain of Sheffield Infirmary in the early 1900s and recalled that

> 'The oldest woman patient in a ward would be affectionately addressed by doctors, nurses and everybody as "Granny" . . . One day, I addressed one such old lady, "Good morning Granny, and how are you today?", when this old damsel of seventy summers pulled herself up straight and with all the dignity she could command, and with a withering glance directed towards myself, retorted, "*My* name is *Miss* Booth." I suppose she was right, but she certainly asserted her old-maidenhood with some vehemence and which the other patients, as I learned afterwards, did not forget to let her know of.'

Three cheers for Miss Booth for refusing to be patronised, but the reaction of her fellow patients is instructive – many single women faced hostility from those around them. Robert Roberts, in *A Ragged Schooling*, recalled that in the Salford slums, 'Many single women,

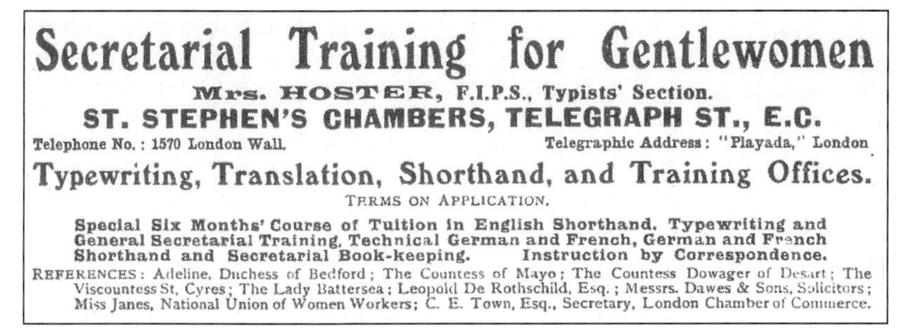

An advertisement from 1915. During the 1800s, 'gentlewomen' could have hoped for only limited working opportunities, such as becoming a governess or a ladies' companion.

middle aged and elderly, through the mere fact of being single had much to put up with from the taunts of youth and the amused contempt of some married neighbours'.

Women outnumbered men (by about half a million in the 1880s, a million and a half by 1900 and two million by the 1920s). The carnage of the First World War created a generation of 'surplus' or 'redundant' women who clung to memories of their soldier sweethearts who never returned – my Great-aunt Florrie lost her betrothed in the war and never married; she spent her life looking after her father and then, when he died and she lost her home, living in as a housekeeper. There is therefore every likelihood that your family will have at least one unmarried daughter in each generation. In 1881, 12 per cent of women aged between 45 and 54 were single. So what did they all do during their lives?

Some, like Great-aunt Florrie, spent the greater part of their lives caring for other members of the family; in fact, one daughter may have been destined to be kept at home for that purpose. In that case, middle class daughters might be rewarded in their father's will by being left sufficient money or property to allow them to live an independent life; if not, they would be thrown onto the jobs market, however ill-prepared they may have been. Working class women like Florrie would usually lose home and support when their parents died, unless someone else in the family took them in.

Until about the 1880s, single middle class women had very limited working opportunities. To become a governess or a teacher, or perhaps a 'lady's companion', was all that was open to the educated female, or she could perhaps open a shop if she had a little capital. Single working class women would work across the spectrum of labour open to their married sisters, although they might look for work that also offered them accommodation, such as living-in domestic service. After the 1880s, horizons began to open considerably for educated women of all classes (though the benefits of universal education took time to percolate down to working class girls). By the 1920s, single women had definite advantages over their married sisters in certain occupations, such as teaching or the civil service, where a marriage bar was operated by employers.

So-called fallen women are, by definition, single women. Illegitimacy is another of those facts of life that family historians have to accept. In many cases, the women concerned subsequently married either the father of the child or someone else. Sometimes, though, they remained single. Whether they made a profession out of their fallen state, or simply struggled on alone, will be something you will have to make a judgement about when you have done some research into her background. Did she, for instance, have just one illegitimate child, or were there several? Did the vicar make a caustic remark in the parish register when he recorded the baptism of yet another 'baseborn' baby? Did she make several stays in the workhouse, where fallen women formed the largest group after the elderly? Pre-1834, under the old poor laws, was she subject of one or more bastardy examinations, or removed from one parish to be sent back to her place of settlement (parish officers were particularly keen to get rid of pregnant women)?

Finding out more

Finding out what happened to your widows and spinsters may once have been low on your priorities as a family historian, but the effort will only enhance your understanding of women's lives and your own family relationships. Sometimes they are easy to keep tabs on, perhaps staying in one parish all their lives. At other times you may need to track them down. *Women alone: Spinsters in England 1650–1850* by

'A Quiet Pipe' at the end of the day.

Bridget Hill (Yale University Press, 2001) is an interesting and informative look at the lives of single women over two centuries and the way that they were viewed by society.

A widow may have moved after her husband's death to stay with one after another of her children or grandchildren. A spinster left at home to look after her parents may also have moved in with another member of the family when they died. One of my spinster ancestors was eventually found living with her great-niece. The **census** will be of major importance (and census indexes even more useful), and you should check **burial registers** in 'family' areas too (pre-1837).

If there are local **almshouses**, check to see if she could have been given accommodation there; records may be with the record office, or if the charity administering the almshouses is still in existence you may have to ask them direct (record office staff may be able to help).

She could be in the union **workhouse** as an old lady, or the local **hospital** after 1930, when the Poor Law gave way to Public Assistance and many workhouses were taken over as hospitals, carrying with them the stigma that was keenly felt amongst the poor. Dread of ending up 'in the workhouse' was not a 19th century phenomenon, there were elderly people who still feared it up until the 1950s or so. A single woman may have been taken into the workhouse if she could not support herself, or if she was pregnant.

Was your widow receiving a **pension**, perhaps from the army if her husband had been a soldier, which would mean that she could be traced through central records? Did she remarry? If you cannot find her death certificate and all trace of her eludes you in the census, consider the possibility and start sifting through parish registers or the General Records Office (GRO) **marriage** indexes.

The **wills** of widows and spinsters are well worth seeking out. Spinsters in particular seem often to have made the effort to remember all family members in their wills, including nieces and nephews and perhaps their children, and even godchildren.

Another possibility for both a widow or spinster who disappears from the usual sources is that she could have **emigrated**. A widow may have had children or grandchildren overseas who invited her to join them, or a single woman may have joined a brother or sister overseas, or simply decided to seek her fortune (and possibly a husband) in the colonies.

5

Passionate Politics and a Public Life

> I say that in a country governed by a woman – where you allow women to form part of the other estate of the realm – peeresses in their own right for example – where you allow a woman not only to hold land, but to be a lady of the manor and hold legal courts – where a woman by law may be a churchwarden and overseer of the poor – I do not see, when she has so much to do with the state and Church, on what reasons, if you come to right, she has not any right to vote. *(Benjamin Disraeli, 1866)*

During the period covered by this book, women entered public life in a way that would have been inconceivable at the beginning of the 19th century – they became councillors and mayors, they sat on school boards and boards of guardians, they voted for their own chosen representatives in Parliament and in local government and they themselves stood for election to those bodies, and they exercised their considerable talents for organisation by supporting charitable causes.

Fighting for the vote

In 1800, however, no woman had the right to vote for her representative in Parliament, and, although over one hundred years later the world had changed almost beyond recognition, that simple fact had not altered.

The Industrial Revolution created not just a new wealthy male middle class, but also wealthy widows and spinster heiresses, who could own property in their own right, and as a result were expected also to pay rates and taxes. But they were not allowed a say in the election of the representatives in Parliament who made the legislation that affected their lives. 'No taxation without representation' had been the cry of the American Revolution only decades before, and it could well have been adopted by the property-owning women of England.

By 1884 the majority of male householders in both urban and rural areas had been granted the vote, so the injustice of exclusion was coming to apply to more and more women. The passing of the Married Women's Property Act in 1882 also had an effect, allowing married women to hold property in their own name. And it was still 'property' that mattered – it was never an objective of the 19th century campaigners to extend the vote to all women, any more than to all men.

Oddly enough, the law itself was in a tangle over women's right to vote. Although there was a strong tradition that they could not vote, there was no actual law on the statute books that forbade it. The Reform Act of 1832 was the first to refer specifically to 'male persons'. And if a woman's name did slip onto an electoral register, by mistake, she was entitled to vote, whatever law or custom might say. If Mrs Lily Maxwell, a Manchester shopkeeper, is your ancestor you will be pleased to know that she is perhaps the first woman to have cast a vote in a parliamentary election. 'It appears,' said *The Times* on 28 November 1867, 'that when a name is on the register the presiding officer has no alternative but to receive the vote of the person who bears the name when it is tendered. . . The name "Lily Maxwell" is registered (no. 12,326) as that of a person entitled to vote for the Parliamentary borough of Manchester. Possibly the registrar may have supposed it to be a masculine name.'

As the 19th century drew to a close, a new generation of women was willing to stand up in public and be counted. In 1892 a huge petition bearing a quarter of a million signatures in support of the female suffrage was handed in to Parliament. In 1897 the National Union of Women's Suffrage Societies was formed under the secretaryship of Millicent Fawcett, bringing together about 500 local societies under one formidable banner.

The violent tactics (towards property, not policemen) of some Suffragettes from 1912 were a great source of social comment for cartoonists, as this postcard shows. (Terry Pankhurst Collection)

A Suffragette demonstration at Hyde Park in 1908. Mrs Emmeline Pankhurst is standing second from left, next to 74 year old Mrs Elizabeth Wolstenholme Elmy, a veteran fighter for women's rights in her native Manchester. (Terry Pankhurst Collection)

The times and the woman came together in Mrs Emmeline Pankhurst. Mrs Pankhurst had a history of militant involvement in the Independent Labour Party. In 1903, impatient with the lack of progress on this one issue of the vote, she and her daughters, Christabel and Sylvia, formed the Women's Social and Political Union (WSPU) and began to galvanise her followers into taking direct action. It was the *Daily Mail* that coined the word 'suffragette' to describe this new breed of woman protester. The Pankhursts, together with Emmeline Pethwick-Lawrence and her husband, made the WSPU into a headline-grabbing phenomenon that combined martyrdom with violence.

The tactics (and the personalities of the leaders) did not please all those who supported the cause, and the breakaway Women's Freedom League (WFL) was formed in 1907. It is worth remembering that many more women belonged to and supported the non-violent, constitutional societies than were ever involved in the suffragette group. They were known as 'suffragists' to distinguish them, and wore the colours green and white, without the purple of the WSPU. It also has to be said that many women opposed both groups, if they cared about the issue at all, and deplored the unwomanly efforts of suffragette and suffragist alike.

Some of the major events of the next few years appear in the timeline at the end of the book, but one tactic which will affect family historians one hundred years later was the call for a female boycott of the 1911 census, taken on the night of 2 April. Many women supporters simply stayed away from home overnight, avoiding the enumerators – 'no vote, no census'. (*Punch* magazine remarked that they must have taken leave of their census.) It will be interesting to see, when the census becomes available in 2012, whether a 'missing' female ancestor is a clue to her involvement in the suffrage movement.

At least that was a peaceful means of protest. During 1913 the suffragette campaign became increasingly violent, with arson attacks and even bomb threats. Did the suffragettes gain women the vote, or did they put back the cause by alienating public opinion? Come to your own conclusions. Whatever the case, the work and responsibility that women took on from 1914 during the First World War meant that the Electoral Reform Act of 1918 at last gave them their due, though only to women aged 30 and over who were eligible ratepayers, the wives of

BOVINGDON POLLING DISTRICT D.			HEMEL HEMPSTEAD DIVISION	
1 **No.**	2 **Names in Full (Surname first).**	3 **Qualifying Premises.**	4 **Description of Service. Ship, Regiment, Number, Rank, Rating, etc., or recorded address.**	5 **No. of Voter on previous Absent Voters' List.**
		PARISH OF FLAUNDEN.		
		FLAUNDEN.		
273	Burgin, Thomas James	110	239744, A. E. Co., 9th Corps	—
274	Burgin, Edward Charles	85	44900 Pte., 2nd Batt. Lincs	828
275	Canziani, Estella L. M.	Oak Cottage	Red Cross V.A.D.	5539
276	Dancer, Thomas	Mill Cottage	120296 Gnr., R.F.A.	5538
277	Jones, Albert Simon	103	46013 Pte., 3rd Batt. Royal Fusiliers	832
278	Jones, Fred	103	179538 Gnr., 17th Batt. R.F.A.	834
279	Mander, Herbert	121	34615 Pte., Somerset L.I.	836
280	Soames, Arthur Granville	Flaunden House	Capt., Coldstream Guards (Inf.)	839
281	Terry, Albert Frederick	Green Dragon	53288 Pte., 2nd Garrison Batt. Northumberland Fusiliers	840

The absent voters' lists are an excellent source for discovering where women were working away from home at the end of the First World War. They can be found in county record offices. (Hertfordshire Archives & Local Studies)

eligible ratepayers, or, in university constituencies, who had, or were eligible for, a degree. In November that year an act allowed women to stand for election to Parliament. Sixteen women candidates stood for the 1919 elections (including Christabel Pankhurst) but the only one to be successful was Countess Markiewicz; as an Irish Republican, standing for Sinn Fein in South Dublin, she never took her seat. However, in a by-election later that year, Nancy Astor became the first woman Member of Parliament. An American heiress and a peer's wife, with no background in the suffrage movement, she was possibly not quite what Mrs Pankhurst had had in mind.

In 1928 full equality with male voters was gained, with the lowering of the age limit to 21 years. At the general election the following year female voters outnumbered men, and the 'flapper vote' (referring to the supposedly frivolous Twenties' girls) was eagerly sought by politicians.

In county and parish

Your ancestor may have voted in local elections or stood for local office long before the parliamentary vote was granted in 1918/1928.

In 1869 an act was passed which gave the municipal vote to women ratepayers of the borough aged 21 and over. A woman's name may therefore appear in local authority electoral registers from 1870, if she owned or occupied a shop or business, or owned her own home. This is likely to apply only to widows and spinsters until 1882, when the Married Women's Property Act provided that a married woman could own property in her own right. At this time, municipal electoral registers were kept separately from those for the parliamentary franchise. After 1919 women of 30 years and over who were married to men entitled to register were also eligible for the local government franchise.

As local ratepayers women were also entitled to vote in elections to, for instance, Poor Law boards of guardians, school boards (after the 1870 Education Act), and county councils (after 1888). When in 1894 parish councils took over parish government from the vestries, all parish ratepayers were entitled to vote in their election.

Although women could serve on school boards or as a member of a board of guardians (Mrs Pankhurst was a Poor Law guardian in

Margaret Bondfield was appointed Minister of Labour in 1929, the first woman to hold a Cabinet position in a British government. The election was the first in which all women over 21 were entitled to vote, the so-called 'Flapper Election'.

Manchester before her days as a suffragette), the women who got the borough vote in 1869 could not stand for election as councillors. In a test case in 1889, following the creation of the London County Council, Lady Sandhurst stood for Brixton and was elected. Following appeals and counter-appeals in the courts (Beresford-Hope v. Lady Sandhurst), she was not allowed to take her seat on the council because she was a woman – something that does not seem to have put off those who voted for her! It was not until 1907 that the Qualification of Women Act enabled women to sit on county or borough councils, or be elected alderman or mayor. In 1908, Dr Elizabeth Garrett-Anderson became the first female mayor in the country, in her home town of Aldeburgh in Suffolk. A decade later, in 1919, the Sex Disqualification Removal Act declared that no one could be 'disqualified by sex or marriage from the exercise of any public function'.

On a parish basis, women who were assessed for the poor rate had for centuries been eligible for appointment to the essential posts that ran the parish – the overseers of the poor, the constables, the surveyors of the highways, the churchwardens and so on. As ratepayers, they could in theory be called on to serve, especially in very small parishes or where it was difficult to find suitable men who would willingly serve their year in office. Such women might serve personally or pay someone to take on some of the duties, but they would still bear the ultimate responsibility for those duties being performed satisfactorily.

This was purely pragmatic and not a recognition of women's equal rights. Serving in parochial office was often not popular.

Charities, societies and the church

Perhaps because women were for so long denied an active political role, they frequently channelled their energies elsewhere and excelled at charitable and fund-raising activities. These might include anything from funding a parish charity or founding almshouses or a school, to organising bazaars or 'fancy fairs'. Many of these worthy women go unrecognised today for the good they did; so if you are lucky enough to find such a woman in your family tree, be sure you do her justice.

One outside body which traditionally attracted female support was the parish church. Here you can find women endowing charities, running Sunday schools, organising and participating in women's societies such as the Mothers' Union, and raising money, as well as arranging the flowers. A group of strong-minded women was perfectly able to run both a vicar and a parish church.

Finding out more

It is certainly worth keeping an open mind and an open eye about the possibility of your female ancestors being involved with political or charitable activities.

If you believe an ancestor was a suffragette, or involved in the **suffrage movement**, first find out more on the background and locality of the various societies involved. *The Women's Suffrage Movement: a Reference Guide 1866–1928* by Elizabeth Crawford (Routledge, 2000) will help you discover what societies may have been active in your area. Records of individuals (other than the principal personalities) will be more difficult to track down. The National Archives has Source Sheet no. 16: Suffragettes, and there was also a useful article on the suffragettes in *Ancestors* magazine (June/July 2002). The Women's Library (Old Castle Street, London E1 7NT; website *www.thewomenslibrary.ac.uk*) holds some original material on societies and individuals. National and local **newspapers** will be helpful, as any suffragette 'outrages' will have been reported and there may also be reports of the meeting of local groups. Don't assume that, because your ancestor lived far from the centre of events in London and the industrial cities, she did not become involved in any way.

Once women had gained the vote, **electoral registers** will be of use from 1919 to trace movement from one address to another, or to make an estimation of the date of death or marriage easier. Much was made in the press of the 1929 election, when women aged 21 and over were able to vote for the first time – you may well find photographs of photogenic young women at the polling booths. One of them might be 'yours'! Residents of a borough entitled to vote in local elections were historically known as burgesses, and so it is **burgess rolls** from after 1869 for which you should look to find the names of women with the municipal vote.

One of the first women to cast her vote in the general election of 14 December 1918.

A female ancestor may have **served** on a school board, a local council, a board of guardians, and so on. Town directories can be helpful, as they often list local representatives. If you then want to take enquiries further, to see what contribution she may have made, look for committee minutes at the county record office. Decisions and quite detailed accounts of meetings were also reported in the local press. A woman who played a part in civic life will also probably warrant a newspaper obituary. Always look at the lists of **parish officers** (churchwardens, overseers, etc.) when you are reading parish papers or local histories, just in case your poor-ratepaying ancestor was pressed into service. Appointments, though possible, were quite unusual, and so may have been reported in the local newspaper.

Do you think that an ancestor endowed a charity, supported a cause, or was a pillar of the local church? There may be **charity boards** hanging in the parish church which will detail benefactors; church guides may also have details. Local histories will certainly mention the charitable founders of almshouses, hospitals or schools. The **Charity Commission** was founded in 1853 and its official reports should cover all charities in the country – see, for instance, the Report of the Commissioners Concerning Charities in England and Wales (the 'Brougham report') of 1894, or the earlier reports of the Commission for Inquiring Concerning Charities, of 1819-40. From 1812 the clerk of the peace in each county was responsible for keeping records of local charities, so mention of them may be made in quarter sessions calendars, which have frequently been printed. County records offices (CROs) may also hold other archive material, perhaps in parish records. Many charities and charitable foundations published **annual yearbooks** or reports. The *Charities Digest* has been published annually since 1882 and lists registered charities; your main reference library should have a current copy and a full set is held at the London Metropolitan Archives (40 Northampton Road, London EC1R 0HB).

Newspapers of the later 19th century and 20th century have many reports of bazaars, charity concerts, fund-raising activities and so on. The women organisers are usually listed by name, as are those who gave money. This source may reveal family connections, or at least show you the circles your ancestor moved in. **Parish magazines**, which can go back as far as the 1880s, are full of information about parish activities and the people involved in them.

CHAPTER 6

Criminal Women

Finding that one of your female ancestors was involved in a crime may be a mixed blessing. There is the benefit of the extra information you could very well uncover about her – you may find a physical description, a photograph, even; you may be able to read a verbatim report of what your ancestor said at the trial; you may discover what she did for a living or how she spent her days. This is information you might never come across otherwise. But then there is the possibility that, having discovered so much, you may not want to share it with too many people. Hence that old joke about the family historian who paid a fortune to trace her family tree, and then another fortune to hush it all up!

Quite a few family historians are proud of their law-breaking ancestors. Having a sheep-stealer in the family – at a safe distance of time, of course – lends a certain excitement to an otherwise dull list of names. But how will you feel about a woman who killed her newborn baby? Or a woman who beat a young servant girl to death after subjecting her to a life of sheer misery? Or a prostitute thief in the family? Men all too often commit unpleasant crimes, but women have a tendency to commit crimes within a smaller world, often within the home or family. You may not always be happy with what you find. This can explain why crimes of past generations are sometimes 'forgotten' by their descendants, or why you come up against an unwillingness to discuss the past when talking to older relatives.

Female crime

Women, of course, in the main followed the same route through the justice system as men. There were, however, certain crimes that were uniquely female or which mainly involved women, and there were some special factors that affected them as criminals and as accessories, victims and witnesses. It is a sad fact that no woman was tried by a jury of her peers until the 20th century, as women were not eligible to sit on a jury, act as counsel or preside as magistrate or judge. Any woman brought before the courts faced an all-male judgement. Most of the time that may not have mattered, but given the prevailing male view of the way women should behave, it must sometimes have mattered a very great deal. Some women were criminalised by their way of life, which could have been forced on them by desertion by their husband or simply by poverty. Prostitutes are mentioned below, but don't forget too the thousands of vagrants who were criminals for the simple fact of homelessness, many of them single women or women with children. 'Vagrant passes' may be found in county record offices.

Infanticide

The killing of a baby by its own mother is always tragic, and some cases are truly moving and pathetic. Until 1803 an iniquitous 17th century law stated that any single woman who had concealed the birth of her illegitimate baby would be presumed guilty of infanticide, if the child was subsequently found dead, and sentenced to death. No proof of her guilt of the crime was required (a married woman, on the other hand, would be presumed innocent until proved guilty). These women were often servants, desperate to conceal a pregnancy that would lose them their job and make it impossible for them to find another.

Understandably, juries had tried to find ways around this verdict, and after 1803 a baby's death was treated as any other case of murder or manslaughter. In 1922 the killing of a newly-born baby by the mother was again made a specific statutory offence of infanticide, and in 1938 the offence was extended to include any child up to the age of twelve months. By this time, recognition of the special nature of this offence meant that if the balance of the mother's mind was considered to be disturbed at the time, she could be charged with the lesser crime of manslaughter – an important distinction when the death penalty was still in force for murder.

Petit treason

When the 19th century dawned, it was only a decade since the official fate of a wife who murdered her husband was to be burned alive (though, by the kindness of the executioner, she might have been strangled or garotted before the flames reached her). Men who murdered their wives, on the other hand, were sentenced to be hanged. The reason for the difference lies in the crime of petit treason.

A wife was considered to owe her husband the same kind of allegiance as a subject owed to his king, and just as the subject could commit treason, so the wife could commit petit (or petty, i.e. small) treason. The same charge would apply to a servant who murdered her employer. In 1790, the penalty for both sexes was made the same – hanging – but it was not until 1828 that the offence of petit treason was abolished.

The attitudes that lay behind the law did not go away so easily. In the criminal courts, it still remained true after 1828 that a husband who killed his adulterous wife might be charged only with manslaughter, while a wife found guilty of murdering her adulterous husband would be hanged for murder.

The law is a ass

You may recall in Charles Dickens' *Oliver Twist* that when Mr and Mrs Bumble are found out in their theft of Oliver's mother's locket, hen-pecked Mr Bumble is told that 'the law supposes that your wife acts under your direction'. '"If the law supposes that," said Mr Bumble, ". . . the law is a ass – a idiot."' A Victorian woman and her husband were indeed considered by the law to be 'one flesh', and the man to be the dominant partner. In criminal cases this had certain effects, which you may come across in your researches.

Under common law, for instance, a wife could not testify for or

THE ILLUSTRATED POLICE NEWS

LAW COURTS AND WEEKLY RECORD

SATURDAY, AUGUST 2, 1879.

PRICE ONE PENNY

EXECUTION OF CATHERINE WEBSTER AT WANDSWORTH GAOL

Catherine (Kate) Webster's execution reported in August 1879. She had murdered her employer Julia Thomas at Richmond, London.

against her husband in a court of law, except if he was accused of assaulting her or of abducting and marrying her against her consent. These exceptions were extended by the 1898 Criminal Evidence Act to include cases of rape, indecent assault, procuration, incest, bigamy, cruelty to children, etc.

A wife could not be charged with being an accessory after the fact for helping her husband to commit a crime, and 'marital coercion' could be used as a defence by a wife caught with her husband and charged with burglary, housebreaking, receiving stolen goods, etc. Only murder and treason were excluded. The inference was that the woman had no mind of her own and was under the influence of her husband. This presumption was abolished in 1925, when actual physical coercion had to be proved.

A husband could not be guilty of the rape of his wife, because her consent was implied when she married him (though he might be guilty of assault). It was not until 1949 that he could be convicted of rape if the couple were legally separated. Less seriously, a wife and husband could not steal from each other. Common law said they were one person and you cannot steal from yourself. The Married Woman's Property Act 1882 made wives responsible for their own financial affairs.

The oldest profession

There is the chance you will come across a prostitute amongst your female ancestors: the *Lancet* in 1857 declared that 'one house in sixty in London is a brothel and one in every sixteen females (of all ages) is, *de facto*, a prostitute'. In villages, you may well be suspicious of the woman who has not one illegitimate child, but two, three or even more. You may also come across a census enumerator who not only knew his area well but was unafraid to call a spade a spade, as in Woodbridge, Suffolk in 1851, when the occupation of Emma Button, Lucy Turner and Sarah Ann Pines, amongst others, was recorded baldly as 'prostitute'.

Prostitution itself, of course, was not a crime, but most of the Victorian female prison population was reckoned to be engaged in the oldest profession. In 1890 Revd G.P. Merrick, chaplain at Millbank

Mrs Savage was convicted of ill-treating her servant, an orphan named Rose Hall, at Norwich in 1876, as reported in the Illustrated Police News.

Prison, conducted a survey of 16,000 such fallen women: 'Almost 6,000 of the women he surveyed had worked as domestic servants, 779 had been barmaids and waitresses and 191 claimed to have been ballet dancers.'! (*Victorian Prison Lives*, see below.)

It was always the woman who got the blame, and rather unfairly prostitutes were blamed for some of the army's failures in the Crimean War. A government commission was appointed in 1857 'to inquire into the sanitary condition of the British Army', and growing concern about the spread of sexually-transmitted disease amongst soldiers and sailors led eventually to the Contagious Diseases Act in 1864. If you have family connections with garrison and naval towns such as Portsmouth, Plymouth, Woolwich, Chatham, Sheerness, Aldershot or Colchester, this act may have affected even your completely respectable female ancestors. The act provided for the compulsory registration, medical examination and treatment of all prostitutes, and cases soon began to be reported in the newspapers of ordinary women in those towns being mistaken for prostitutes by the authorities and subjected to manhandling. The unfairness of the act, which left the male customers unmolested, and the degrading forced treatment that the act sanctioned produced one of the fiercest battles of the sexes of the Victorian era. Mrs Josephine Butler rose to prominence as the leader of a campaign to have the act repealed. In 1883 compulsory medical examination was ended and three years later the act was repealed. Meanwhile, Josephine Butler and her campaigners brought other evils into the public eye, including the 'white slave' scandal of British women kept against their will in Continental brothels and child prostitution.

Trevor Fisher's *Prostitution and the Victorians* (Sutton, 1997) gives a good overview of the subject with much contemporary evidence.

Prison, transportation or the gallows?

When sentence was passed and the trial was over, what faced your ancestor then? Summary trial before the magistrates might result in a fine or a short period in gaol. Being found guilty of an offence at the quarter sessions or assizes, however, might lead to prison, transportation to the colonies, or the gallows.

Early 19th century gaols were the stuff of nightmares: dark and filthy places in which people were kept in medieval conditions. When Mrs Elizabeth Fry first visited the women prisoners in Newgate prison in 1813, she found appalling scenes of violence and despair. Her reforming work and the changes urged by the Prison Discipline Society helped to make improvement possible by the 1830s, with the appointment of prison inspectors and the separation of the sexes. New government prisons were planned and built; Millbank was the first in 1816. Most women prisoners were housed in separate wings of predominantly male prisons such as Millbank, before being sent to Brixton

Sarah Martin (1791–1843), daughter of a Norfolk tradesman, taught the scriptures and handicrafts to prisoners in Yarmouth gaol and helped many to find employment when freed. Her story appeared in the Victorian book, The Lives of Good and Great Women.

Women prisoners, with their babies, exercising at Wormwood Scrubs in the 1900s (from George Sims' Living London*).*

or Fulham Women's Prison (built as a reformatory in 1853 and made a prison in 1864; it closed in 1888). Holloway Prison only became exclusively female in 1902. *Victorian Prison Lives* by Philip Priestley (Pimlico, 1999) is excellent background reading.

Transportation to Australia may not have seemed such a bad alternative: the sentence was imposed for a minimum of five years, depending on the crime. Not all criminals sentenced to transportation actually left the country and sometimes you may find an ancestor serving their sentence in England instead. After 1857 transportation was not commonly used as a sentence and it was completely abolished in 1868; in practice, transportation for women had ceased decades before. David Hawkings' *Bound for Australia* (Phillimore, 1987) is a good introduction to the topic. Australian family history societies have an interest in this subject, not surprisingly, and it may be useful to contact (or join) the one covering the area your ancestor went to. Outside our period, but fascinating, is Sian Rees's *The Floating Brothel* (Headline, 2001).

If it was the man of the family who was transported, there may be a petition from his wife, pleading for his sentence to be reduced to one of imprisonment, preserved amongst Home Office records. Families could be left destitute if the wage-earning husband was taken away, and it was really quite unlikely that he would ever return. Many women were left in the position of my ancestor Ann Loom, whose husband was transported for sheepstealing in the 1830s. She obviously took up with a local man, David Broom, and is recorded in the census as his 'housekeeper', although the family of illegitimate children she produced also lived with the couple. What choice did she have? She was left in limbo, not single, a wife or widow but expected to look after herself. If you have a male transportee in the family, don't forget to check what happened to his family left behind.

At the beginning of the 19th century there were about 200 offences for which your ancestor could have been sentenced to death, some of them incredibly petty and most related to forms of theft. Every sentence of death had to be confirmed by the monarch, who could also commute the sentence to transportation or imprisonment – six long weeks might go by after the trial before word was received that she was saved or would hang. By the 1830s the death penalty had been repealed for most of those offences, and in fact after 1841 executions were for murder only. (The last woman to be hanged for murder in this country was Ruth Ellis in 1955.)

Finding out more

Criminal Ancestors by David Hawkings (Sutton, revised edition, 1996) is essential reading if you do find a criminal in your family. It explains in depth the background to the court and punishment systems and has examples of many different documents so that you can see what you may be lucky enough to find at record offices or the National Archives (PRO). There are always new developments on the Internet, too – if your ancestor appeared in the dock at the **Old Bailey** in London between 1670 and 1834, for instance, you can find full details of the trial on the Internet at *www.oldbaileyonline.org*.

If your ancestor was caught up in an interesting case, her name may very well appear in local **newspapers**. Cases that were out of the ordinary in any way – particularly gory, sexual, or amusing perhaps – would have been picked up by the national press, just as they are today. **Local history** books often mention murders or other notorious crimes, sometimes in depth; murder also has a literature all its own and many cases do get written about at length.

Lastly, a gravestone or other memorial for an ancestor may throw up a gem. In 1883 William Andrews noted a moral lesson in stone at Bury St Edmunds (quoted by Nigel Rees, *Epitaphs*, 1993):

> Reader/Pause at this Humble Stone/it Records/The fall of unguarded Youth/By the allurements of vice/and the treacherous snares of Seduction/Sarah Lloyd/on the 23d of April 1800, /in the 22d Year of her Age,/Suffered a Just but ignominious/ Death/for admitting her abandoned seducer/into the Dwelling House of/her Mistress,/in the Night of 3d Oct/1799/and becoming the Instrument/in his Hands of the crimes/of Robbery and House-burning./These were her last Words:/May my example be a/warning to Thousands.

CHAPTER 7

A Working Life

Women in your family tree may have been coalminers or nailmakers, parlourmaids or dressmakers, doctors or lawyers, teachers or cotton weavers. The great majority of our female ancestors worked for their living at some time in their lives (women with private means and those who moved smoothly from dependence on a middle-class father to a middle-class husband excepted). Yet there is often little evidence to show what work they did; if there is therefore a tendency to dismiss the subject as of little interest, it does not do justice to those hard-working women. Over the 150 years from 1800 to 1950 women may be found in every corner of agriculture, heavy and light industry, manufacture, the service industries and the professions. From the lowliest skivvy to the qualified surgeon, they all deserve recognition.

Women at work

Few early or mid-Victorian girls could expect a better or more fulfilling working life than their mothers had. A girl was expected to be trained primarily in domestic skills such as cooking and sewing, which would fit her for the married home life she would surely achieve – or domestic work if she did not. Middle class girls might fare better in the education paid for by their fathers, perhaps at a private academy or with a governess, but for them too intellectual skills were not highly prized and might even be seen as a positive drawback in the contest to make a suitable match, while accomplishments such as drawing, playing the piano or French conversation would be much more useful. Even when university education became a possibility for a few middle class girls in the early 1900s, they usually had to face the fact that a higher education meant a lower expectation of ever getting married. Progress was slow in persuading the male universities to take women students seriously – it was not until 1920 that they were admitted to full membership of Oxford University, and Cambridge University resisted until 1948.

For the majority of the women in our families higher education was hardly an option until after the Second World War, and the lives of working class women tended to follow a pattern. When a girl left school she would immediately look for work, perhaps as a domestic servant or in a local factory. Unlike her brothers, she would not be particularly concerned about a job with prospects as her expectation would be to marry and raise a family. If marriage did not materialise by the time she was in her late twenties, she might have to look for a job with more security or one that provided board and lodging, such as live-in domestic service or shopwork. If married, she would probably leave full-time work to raise her children, taking on casual work as and when she could manage it. When the oldest child could be left to look after the rest, she would look for steadier work, and she would then probably undertake some form of work for the rest of her life – there were no old age pensions until 1909. And whatever work she did during her life, she could be sure that her wage would always be less than the pay received by fellow male workers.

In the professions working after marriage was forbidden. A marriage bar was actually imposed by employers. In *Out of the Doll's House* (BBC Books, 1988), Angela Holdsworth relates the story of Janet Young, who married in 1935 while working for the Bank of England. She could not afford to lose her job, so she kept her marriage secret, even from family and friends. In 1938 she married her husband again, this time publicly. Janet's two marriage certificates are reproduced in the book – a puzzle solved for some future genealogist!

'The freedom of the house' also meant no servants in the 1920s. Advertisements can sometimes encapsulate social change in few words!

Women's work?

During the 19th century, as agriculture declined as a major employer of women, domestic service and factory work absorbed most of the female working population. Women in some areas worked at home in craft industries such as straw plaiting, lacemaking, glove making, etc. In agricultural areas, little changed for women until after the Second World War. In the village of Abbotts Ann after the First World War, one Hampshire woman remembered, 'When girls left school there was little to do but go into service. If they did not have a live-in position they had to walk, often for miles, to be there on duty at 6.30 am. Married women did casual farm work and gathered flints from the fields for the road surfacing.' (*Hampshire Within Living Memory*, Countryside Books, 1994.) It was little different from the choice that faced their Victorian grandmothers. Where your family lived will have influenced the work the women did. Local history research will tell you what work was

Girls making artificial flowers at home in the early 1900s.

important in your area – a cotton mill, perhaps, or a craft industry such as glovemaking.

When you are thinking about local industries and employers, do not discount possible areas of employment because they do not seem 'female'. Women worked in many physically demanding industries in the 19th century, such as coal mines, slate quarries, engineering works, brickfields, salt works, etc. The Wigan pit brow girls are a good example. In 1842 the employment of women and children underground in coal mines was prohibited, but this did not stop women from working on the surface, at the pit brow. A long campaign waged by the miners' trade unions against the women was unsuccessful, and they were still shifting tons of coal in the third quarter of the 19th century.

Similarly, try not to make assumptions that jobs thought of today as typically female – such as hairdressing or secretarial work – were seen as such in the 1800s. Hairdressers were usually male until at least the 1870s, and the first secretaries were men, not women. Nursing is another job that has undergone a change since 1800, when a nurse would often have been a slovenly, untrained attendant rather than the uniformed, antiseptic and hard working 'angel of the sick room' she became within the century.

It can also be helpful to consider family ties and traditions in deciding a young girl's future. Beatrice Sellers recalled that in the 1920s at Ramsbottom in Lancashire 'parents stuck to the idea that if one member of the family went into the mill, all the rest did the same. My mother would have liked to be a teacher . . . but when the head teacher went to see my grandmother to ask her permission for my mother to be trained, Grandma said that all her sisters worked in the mill and she would have to do the same'. (*Lancashire Within Living Memory*, Countryside Books, 1997.) No chance, then, of one of the family getting above her station. A very wide gap existed between those at the top and bottom of society and the gradations in between were many: 'knowing your place' was an inhibitor on many young women who dreamed of a more fulfilling life.

Scenes from 'the horrors of the coal mines' before women were banned from working underground in 1842 (from The Life and Work of the Seventh Earl of Shaftesbury, *1893).*

Finding out more

How do you find out what work your female ancestors did for a living? **Census returns** may help, but they only give a snapshot of life every ten years and do not record all women's work, simply because so much of it was seasonal or part time, such as pea-picking or harvesting. A very full and busy working life may also be concealed beneath a category such as 'farmer's wife' or 'innkeeper's wife'. **Civil registration** certificates may give clues, though again, as with the census, women's occupations may not be recorded.

Otherwise, hints may be picked up if she ever came up against bureaucracy – perhaps in **poor law** or **criminal** records. **Trade directories** may also be useful as they should list women who had their own businesses, such as milliners or shopkeepers, or, in the 20th century, provided professional services such as chiropody or dentistry. Above all, talk to the **family** – they may well remember hearing tales of life below stairs or as a mill girl from elderly relatives.

You may find it difficult, if not impossible, to discover much about your individual female ancestors' working lives. Having said that, though, there is a great deal of interesting information that can be gleaned from filling in the background. It is not possible to mention more than a few of the more obvious areas of work here.

***On the land*:** Women have worked on the land for centuries, as the wives and daughters of farmers, as labourers, or as farmers in their own right. Some areas of farming, such as dairying, were a female preserve, and a good dairymaid was sought after and well worth her wage to her employer. However, as the 19th century progressed, working in the fields came to be seen as unfeminine. In 1851, 144,000 women were recorded as working on the land, but 30 years later the figure had fallen to only 40,000. This was partly due to the increasing mechanisation of farmwork, which affected many of the labour-intensive jobs previously done by women, and also because the women themselves felt that working in the fields was no longer a suitably respectable job – what Flora Thompson called 'a distaste for "goin' afield" '. Women did, however, still take on seasonal work such as fruit or hop picking, which

'A gang in the Fens – early morning'. Agricultural 'gangs' of women and young people became notorious in the later 1800s and this drawing by R. W. Macbeth from the English Illustrated Magazine *in 1885 seems to emphasise the menace of the male gang leaders.*

might form an important part of the annual family budget.

Researching individual women farm workers may prove impossible and you may just have to be satisfied with discovering what life was like for female agricultural workers in the area. For an introduction, read *Labouring Life in the Victorian Countryside* by Pamela Horn (Alan Sutton, 1987) or *The English Countrywoman* by G.E. and K.R. Fussell (Orbis, 1981), and there are many other good general books on rural life to be sought out; for something more specific to your locality find out from the library what has been published by museums or local history societies, for instance. There were several parliamentary enquiries into agricultural working life during the 19th century, which often yield first-hand accounts of what life was like in the fields. You can order copies of such papers through your reference library system; for the titles and dates of the various commissions see books by P. & G. Ford, published by Southampton University Studies: *Hansard's Breviate of British Parliamentary Papers to 1833* and *Select List of British Parliamentary Papers 1833–1890.*

Domestic service: In 1861 over two and a half million women were in paid employment, about a quarter of the female population. Of these, two million were in domestic service, which would remain the largest employer of women, particularly from rural areas, until the Second World War. Even in the 1920s, one in three women were working as domestic servants – being able to employ even one young girl as a maid of all work was still a status symbol beloved of middle class families. There can be few, if any, families without at least one servant in their family tree.

It is ironic that despite the huge numbers of women involved, it will normally be very difficult to find records relating to women in domestic service, as so many of them worked for private families. For instance, I know from the 1881 census that a three-times great-aunt was a 'cook general' in London (i.e. a cook working in a small household, probably doing some domestic duties as well) but where she worked is impossible to discover. If she had worked at the 'big house' in a rural area, however, I might have had better luck. Estate or household records, which may yield servants' names and wages, sometimes survive, perhaps held by the county record office or still in private hands.

You can read up on the background, with plenty of illustrative detail, in books such as Pamela Horn's *The Rise and Fall of the Victorian Servant* (Alan Sutton, 1995) or, concisely, *The Victorian Domestic Servant* by Trevor May (Shire, 2001). Contemporary books such as Mrs Beeton's *Book of Household Management* (1859–61; facsimile first edition Chancellor Press, 1982) have interesting directions as to the duties of domestic servants.

***Factory and office work*:** Working in a factory could cover anything from cotton spinning to decorating chinaware. While domestic service was the biggest employer of women at the end of the 19th century, the textile and clothing trades employed most of the rest of the female working population. Office work, too, expanded greatly over the last decades of the 1800s, particularly for female clerks and typists, and there was a demand for female telephonists.

Researching a particular firm, factory or industry may be possible and business archives have sometimes been deposited with record offices. You may find wages books, photographs, firm histories, newsletters, etc. Local museums should be able to tell you about large employers in the area, and some companies even have their own archives and museum.

'A charming little maid' – my grandmother recalled such episodes with considerably less affection, but unwanted attention from the man of the house could be something of an occupational hazard.

Nursing**:** Several large hospitals established nurse training schools in the 19th century, the first being Florence Nightingale's school at St Thomas's in London. In 1916 the Royal College of Nursing was formed, and since 1921 nurses have had to be registered; the records are held at the National Archives. Midwives have been registered since 1902. The history of military nursing is touched on in Chapter 8.

Hospital records may be useful, as some will relate to individual staff. Visit the website of the Hospital Records Database, a joint project between the Wellcome Institute and the National Archives, which makes it easy to discover where records are held (*http://hospitalrecords.pro.gov.uk*). You may also find some information about nurses employed in workhouses amongst Poor Law papers created by boards of guardians, or at the National Archives in registers of paid union officers. Many hospitals have had histories published which give a great deal of information about staff and working conditions, such as *The Central Middlesex Hospital; the first 60 years 1903-1963* by J.D. Allan Grey (Pitman Medical Publishing, 1963). Some hospitals have their own archives and museums, such as St Bartholomew's in London (*www.bartsandthelondon.org.uk*).

Teaching**:** Until the 1840s no training or experience was required to open or teach in a school, but in 1846 the government stepped in and created 'apprenticeships' of five years as a pupil-teacher, with an examination at the end for entry to training college, although not all teachers chose to take the examinations – Pamela Horn, in *The Victorian and Edwardian Schoolchild*, quotes the figure of 41 per cent of teachers as being uncertificated in 1914. After 1870 demand for trained teachers grew tremendously and the profession came to be staffed mainly by women, who were paid much less than their male counterparts. The Teachers Registration Council kept records of teachers registered since 1902 (the Society of Genealogists may be able to help with specific queries), but it is not easy to find personal records of teachers generally during the 20th century. Sometimes school records can help, if you know where she taught. As with nurses, 19th century teachers may appear in Poor Law records, and there could be information in the records of school boards (after 1870) and local education authorities (after 1902).

It seems likely that this undated photograph shows nurses newly qualified and keen to record their achivement.

Doctors**:** In 1859 Bristol-born Elizabeth Blackwell became the first woman to have her name included on the British Medical Register, though she had to qualify in America. In 1865 Elizabeth Garrett succeeded in getting her name onto the register after she qualified by diploma from the Society of Apothecaries. The struggle by women doctors to gain acceptance by the medical profession was a long one and sometimes distinctly ill-natured – Sir William Jenner in 1878 declared that he would rather see his daughter dead than a medical student. In 1876 medical licensing bodies were required to open their examinations to women, but only at their discretion. By 1900 about 200 women had qualified as medical practitioners, and most of those worked in the cities. By the 1930s, there were about 8,500 women doctors.

Medical registers will list your ancestor if she qualified as a doctor; many registers are available at the Society of Genealogists. *Records of the Medical Profession* by S. Bourne and A.H. Chicken (Bourne & Chicken, 1994) will be of help if you want to look into the background in more detail. Hospital records (see above) may hold information on individual doctors, if you know where she worked.

A few more ideas:

There are occupational indexes being created all the time. See *Specialist Indexes for Family Historians* by Jeremy Gibson and Elizabeth Hampson (FFHS, 2nd edition, 2000) for ideas, and keep up to date by reading one of the family history magazines (see Appendix). And, lastly, a few things to think about: **Apprenticeship records** do not deal only with male apprentices – girls too could be apprenticed to a trade, sometimes at quite a distance from their home. Many women took over their husband's or father's **business** when he died, or they may have run a business on their own, and you quite often find reference in trade directories to women running inns and beerhouses, as well as all kinds of shops. Licensing records will be helpful for innkeepers; a pubs, inns and tavern index is being created on the internet (*www.pubsindex.freeserve.co.uk*) listing licensees from 1801 to 1901. Women traders could go **bankrupt**. The *Daily Mail Yearbook* for 1915 recorded that the 'total number of women who failed in 1913 was 355; of these 36 were milliners and dressmakers'. Bankruptcy records are held at the National Archives, and bankruptcy proceedings will be recorded in the *London Gazette*, *The Times* or the local press.

Trade union records may sometimes be useful for background on a particular trade or industry or if you know that your ancestor was active in a union. There was a great deal of male trade union opposition to women workers during the 19th century and during the two world wars, and many unions refused to accept female members. In 1874 the Women's Protective and Provident League was formed (later, the Women's Trade Union League) to help small unions of women and to campaign for protective legislation. By the late 19th century there were several instances when women struck for better pay and conditions, notably the Bryant and May matchgirls in 1888. Unions continued to

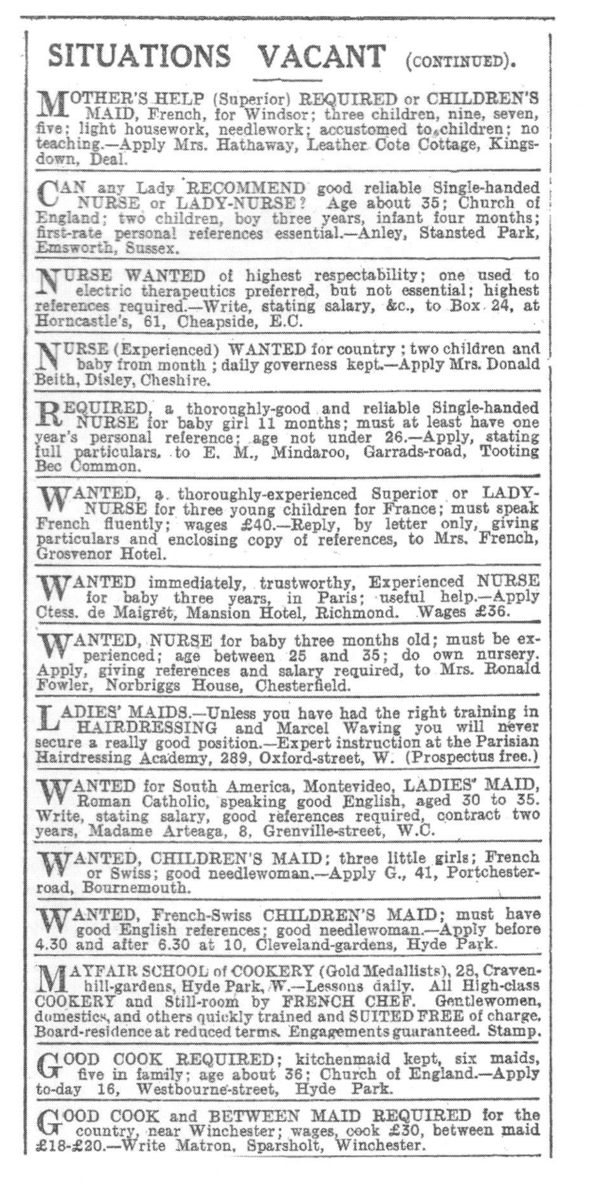

SITUATIONS VACANT (CONTINUED).

MOTHER'S HELP (Superior) REQUIRED or CHILDREN'S MAID, French, for Windsor; three children, nine, seven, five; light housework, needlework; accustomed to children; no teaching.—Apply Mrs. Hathaway, Leather Cote Cottage, Kingsdown, Deal.

CAN any Lady RECOMMEND good reliable Single-handed NURSE or LADY-NURSE? Age about 35; Church of England; two children, boy three years, infant four months; first-rate personal references essential.—Anley, Stansted Park, Emsworth, Sussex.

NURSE WANTED of highest respectability; one used to electric therapeutics preferred, but not essential; highest references required.—Write, stating salary, &c., to Box 24, at Horncastle's, 61, Cheapside, E.C.

NURSE (Experienced) WANTED for country; two children and baby from month; daily governess kept.—Apply Mrs. Donald Beith, Disley, Cheshire.

REQUIRED, a thoroughly-good and reliable Single-handed NURSE for baby girl 11 months; must at least have one year's personal reference; age not under 26.—Apply, stating full particulars, to E. M., Mindaroo, Garrads-road, Tooting Bec Common.

WANTED, a thoroughly-experienced Superior or LADY-NURSE for three young children for France; must speak French fluently; wages £40.—Reply, by letter only, giving particulars and enclosing copy of references, to Mrs. French, Grosvenor Hotel.

WANTED immediately, trustworthy, Experienced NURSE for baby three years, in Paris; useful help.—Apply Ctess. de Maigrét, Mansion Hotel, Richmond. Wages £36.

WANTED, NURSE for baby three months old; must be experienced; age between 25 and 35; do own nursery. Apply, giving references and salary required, to Mrs. Ronald Fowler, Norbriggs House, Chesterfield.

LADIES' MAIDS.—Unless you have had the right training in HAIRDRESSING and Marcel Waving you will never secure a really good position.—Expert instruction at the Parisian Hairdressing Academy, 289, Oxford-street, W. (Prospectus free.)

WANTED for South America, Montevideo, LADIES' MAID, Roman Catholic, speaking good English, aged 30 to 35. Write, stating salary, good references required, contract two years, Madame Arteaga, 8, Grenville-street, W.C.

WANTED, CHILDREN'S MAID; three little girls; French or Swiss; good needlewoman.—Apply G., 41, Portchester-road, Bournemouth.

WANTED, French-Swiss CHILDREN'S MAID; must have good English references; good needlewoman.—Apply before 4.30 and after 6.30 at 10, Cleveland-gardens, Hyde Park.

MAYFAIR SCHOOL of COOKERY (Gold Medallists), 28, Craven-hill-gardens, Hyde Park, W.—Lessons daily. All High-class COOKERY and Still-room by FRENCH CHEF. Gentlewomen, domestics, and others quickly trained and SUITED FREE of charge. Board-residence at reduced terms. Engagements guaranteed. Stamp.

GOOD COOK REQUIRED; kitchenmaid kept, six maids, five in family; age about 36; Church of England.—Apply to-day 16, Westbourne-street, Hyde Park.

GOOD COOK and BETWEEN MAID REQUIRED for the country, near Winchester; wages, cook £30, between maid £18-£20.—Write Matron, Sparsholt, Winchester.

Newspaper 'small ads' are useful for background information on wages and conditions. These appeared in the Morning Post, *25 September 1914.*

develop on single-sex lines. In 1906 the National Federation of Women Workers was formed to help especially exploited home workers; from 1906 to 1914 female union membership more than doubled to over 350,000. It is not easy to trace trade union records, especially since so many smaller unions have been taken over and amalgamated over the years; *Nineteenth Century Trade Union Records: an Introduction and Select Guide* by H. Southall, D. Gilbert and C. Bryce (Historical Geography Research Series, 1994) is a useful introduction.

The small ads of **newspapers**, including the national papers, from about the 1880s onward, can be useful for background information such as current rates of pay and what kind of employee the advertisers were looking for. There is also a wide range of trade journals and many examples can be found at the British Library.

Photographic collections have been made of women workers – for example, Frank Meadow Sutcliffe's photographs of fisherwomen on the Yorkshire coast held at the Sutcliffe Museum, Whitby, and Horace Nicholl's photographs of First World War workers, held at the Imperial War Museum. An interesting book containing many photographs of working class women collected by Arthur Munby is *Victorian Working Women: Portraits from Life* by Michael Hiley (Gordon Fraser Gallery, 1979).

And don't assume she would have stayed in one place. Some women **travelled** long distances for work even in the 19th century. Pit bank girls from Shropshire, for instance, walked down to the market gardens just outside London every May. They picked and carried fruit and vegetables for the summer and returned home in the autumn. (Once canal or railway travel became possible, life was somewhat easier!) 'In 1822 a Wellington girl gave birth at the poor house to an illegitimate son whose father was a maltman from Fulham, and in 1824 another was delivered of the child of a bricklayer from High Holborn.' (*The Industrial Revolution in Shropshire* by Barrie Trinder, Phillimore, 2000.) Another genealogical mystery solved?

CHAPTER 8

Women and War

'My Gawd, it's a woman!' A wounded First World War soldier's bewildered reaction on coming round to find that a female ambulance driver was bending over him sums up the response of most men to the arrival of women at the front line. Many books have been written about the battlefields of the Western Front, the appalling suffering of the trenches, the terrible casualties. Many family historians research their First World War ancestors. But relatively few think to research the wartime experiences of the female members of the family.

Wives and nurses

Your several times great-grandmother may have been with Wellington's army when they fought Napoleon's troops in the Peninsular War, but sadly it is highly unlikely that you will ever know – the records simply do not exist. The army trailed in its wake a large number of camp followers and a smaller number of soldiers' wives, but very few were officially recorded. In 1811 the Duke of York issued orders that only 'six lawful wives of soldiers were permitted to embark on Active Foreign Service with every 100 men', but women often simply attached themselves to the regiment their man was serving in and followed it anyway, relying on scavenging off the countryside and battlefield plunder for their survival. They were, according to the historian Charles Oman, 'an extraordinary community – hard as nails, expert plunderers,

Soldiers' wives and women have always followed their men, officially or not. The chance of tracing them, however, is not great.

furious partisans of the supreme excellence of their own battalion, much given to fighting' (quoted in *Judy O'Grady and the Colonel's Lady*, see below). It makes you want to find one in your family tree, doesn't it!

In war and peace, women cooked, cleaned and washed for their soldier husbands and for the officers of the regiment. A few wives were employed in regimental hospitals as matrons and head nurses, though nursing the sick and wounded was then carried out mainly by male orderlies. Florence Nightingale's party of nurses arriving in the Crimea in 1854 was not therefore a completely revolutionary event, except that they were unrelated to the army and many of them were more genteelly born than run-of-the-mill nurses of the time, who were generally perceived as an unsavoury lot and definitely working class.

Despite the public acclaim that greeted Nightingale's nurses on their return to England and the work that Florence herself persevered in to make nursing a respectable and respected profession, change within the army was extremely slow. A handful of female nurses were employed at the military hospitals in Chatham, London, Netley and Woolwich, but over 20 years passed before the Army Nursing Service (ANS) was formed in 1881. Military nursing proved an attractive proposition for many young women seeking a more responsible and adventurous life, and during the South African War (1899-1902) over a thousand ANS sisters served in Africa with the army. In 1902 the Army Nursing Service was renamed Queen Alexandra's Imperial Military Nursing Service. In 1908 the Territorial Force Nursing Service (TFNS) was formed (renamed the Territorial Army Nursing Service in 1921).

The situation in the navy was slightly different. Only in 1884 were female nurses first employed in naval hospitals, when a few were appointed to the naval hospital at Haslar. Up until then sick or wounded sailors had been nursed by sailors' wives or male naval pensioners. In 1902 the service became known as Queen Alexandra's Royal Naval Nursing Service (QARNNS).

Twentieth century world war

The two world wars of the 20th century involved women in ways that would have seemed unthinkable in Victorian times. Although non-combatants, they served in the armed forces alongside male servicemen and at home faced death, destruction and the stress of coping in a society under attack.

The First World War

When the First World War broke out, many women who offered their services to their country were dismissed out of hand. 'My good lady, go home and sit still,' Dr Elsie Inglis was told when she suggested a military hospital staffed by female doctors, while Vera Laughton Matthews was told by the Admiralty, 'We don't want any petticoats here.' Neither took much notice – Dr Inglis founded the Scottish Field Hospitals and Vera Matthews formed the first WRNS unit and went on to become director of the service in 1939.

This reluctance to accept female volunteers did not apply to nurses, of course. When war broke out in 1914 the military nursing service was able immediately to go into action, its small peacetime numbers (about

300) rapidly supplemented by calling up the reserves. Over 2,000 nurses signed up for the reserve in 1914, and by 1919 there were over 10,000 qualified serving sisters. During the war they staffed and ran base hospitals, casualty clearing stations and advanced operating centres, often within a bomb's fall of the front line. Amazingly, casualties amongst the nurses themselves were light.

Untrained civilians were encouraged to enrol as members of the Voluntary Aid Detachment (VAD) under the auspices of the British Red Cross Society and Order of St John, which had joined together 'for the duration'. The VAD had first been formed in 1909 in connection with the Territorial Force Nursing Service, and in 1914 about 47,000 women volunteered. Over the next four years they worked in hospitals at home, at the front and on board ship, staffed dressing stations, cooked, cleaned, nursed the sick and drove ambulances. It is thought that about 126,000 female VADs were employed during the course of the war.

Also loosely connected with the nursing service, though not within its control and not officially part of the military, were the splendidly individualistic volunteer members of the First Aid Nursing Yeomanry (FANY). Although their eccentric founder in 1907 had envisaged a troop of nurses on horseback (hence 'Yeomanry'), they in fact drove ambulances and other vehicles. They were cold-shouldered by the military authorities at the start of the war, so they simply crossed the Channel and went to work for the Belgians, who welcomed them. The women, few in number, came to be recognised for their bravery and energy. One of them was Muriel Thompson, the first British woman racing driver.

By 1916 the need to replace men killed or wounded at the Front was becoming imperative and forced the authorities to rethink their attitude to women in the forces. The army agreed to take on women to staff areas behind the lines, and the first members of the new Women's Army Auxiliary Corps (WAAC; renamed Queen Mary's AAC in April 1918) arrived in France in 1917. About 57,000 women served in the WAAC during the war. Members of the Women's Legion, founded at the start of the war, were admitted as drivers with the Royal Army Service Corps and the Royal Flying Corps, and acted as dispatch riders.

The newly formed Royal Air Force had its own nursing service from early 1918, with 130 sisters by 1919. Also in 1918, on 1 April, women

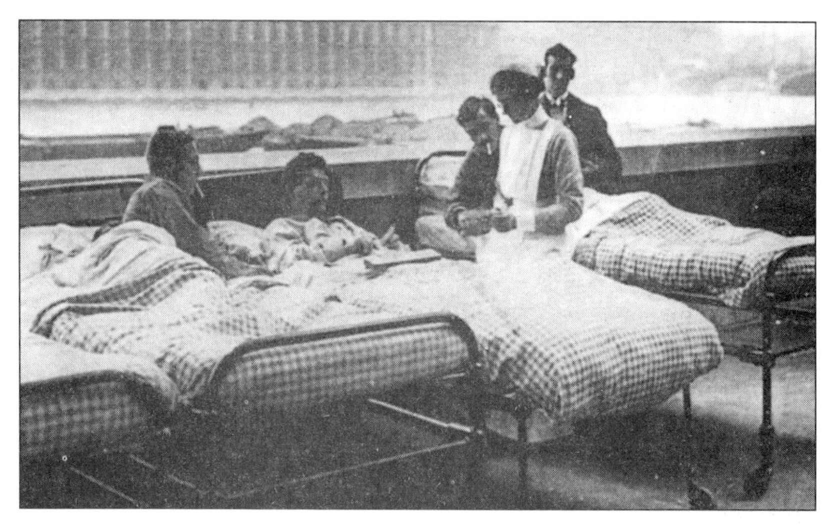

Nursing wounded soldiers on the terrace at St Thomas's Hospital, London (pictured in the Sphere, *June 1915).*

from the WAAC and the WRNS were transferred to form a new service – the Women's Royal Air Force (WRAF) – which took over some non-combatant duties. The Royal Navy had formed its own women's service in November 1917 – the Women's Royal Naval Service (WRNS) – although women had been filling support roles since 1916. 'Free a man for sea service' was the slogan that encouraged women to join. About 25,000 women served in the WRAF and 6,000 in the WRNS.

The Second World War

When war came again in 1939 women were once more called upon to 'free the men for action', and two years later the conscription of women was agreed to by Parliament for the first time. The second National Service Act in 1941 made service compulsory for single women and childless widows between the ages of 20 and 25, later expanded to 19 to 30. Servicewomen also became eligible for all the traditional decorations that had hitherto been awarded to men only, including the Victoria Cross.

The Women's Royal Naval Service (WRNS) was formed in 1939, the only women's service to use a title already proven during the First World War, although it proved also to be the only women's service that was not granted equivalent status in rank to male colleagues. In a gradual mobilisation of volunteers, the Wrens took on jobs such as cooks or stewards, office work, communications, radar, aircraft mechanics at naval air stations, maintenance of torpedoes, boarding officers and boat crew. In 1941 the first Wrens went overseas, to Singapore. About 100,000 women saw service with the WRNS during the war.

The Auxiliary Territorial Service (ATS) was formed in 1938, specifically to work with the army, and by September 1939 17,000 women had enlisted. Their most famous recruit was Princess Elizabeth, but '[w]omen from every walk of life were joining – housewives, many with husbands in the forces, shop assistants, secretaries, mannequins, beauty specialists, university women, women with business careers, women whose interests had centred wholly on home life', said a post-war publication, *Women in Uniform* by D. Collett Wadge (Sampson Low, Marston & Co., 1946).

By 1943 there were 212,000 women in the ATS, including, among 80 different occupations, skilled tradeswomen, clerks, switchboard operators, cooks, orderlies, batwomen, drivers and members of the blood transfusion service. Some worked with REME, others with the Royal Corps of Signals – they went wherever they were needed in support of the army. The first mixed searchlight regiment was formed in 1942, and women performed a hugely important role in the protection of English towns and cities against bomber attack. 'The girls lived like men, fought their lights like men, and, alas, some of them died like men,' said General Sir Frederick Pile, C.-in-C. of Anti-Aircraft Command. Lance Corporal Grace Catherine Golland, for instance, was awarded the British Empire Medal in 1944 for her courage when 'she was engulfed by smoke and flame from some 50 IBs [incendiary bombs] which landed close to her, accompanied by HE [high explosive] bombs which killed cattle in the next field'. 'Despite the concussion from bombs and the heat and fumes engendered by the incendiaries, Lance Corporal Golland remained at her post and by her coolness and leadership enabled her team to maintain their duties, thereby allowing the site to fire in further engagements in a period of 57 minutes.'

The Women's Auxiliary Air Force (WAAF) was formed originally as 48 RAF companies within the ATS, which transferred to the RAF in 1939. By late 1943 there were 182,000 women in the service, about 16 per cent of the total strength of the RAF. They served in all RAF commands and all over the world. Members included air ambulance orderlies, armourers, balloon operators, photographic interpretors, flight mechanics, radar operators, etc., plus all the usual clerical and domestic trades.

From 1940 women were admitted to the Air Transport Auxiliary (ATA), ferrying aircraft from factory to aerodrome. It was work that attracted independent-minded women fliers. Perhaps the most famous was Mrs Amy Johnson Mollison, who in the 1930s had been the first woman to fly solo from England to Australia; she died in January 1941, when the plane she was ferrying crashed in the Thames estuary. The women pilots were given equal pay and status with men in late 1943 and flew all kinds of planes, including four-engined bombers. About 900 women also worked as ground staff.

Nurses were of course in great demand and VADs were once again in action with all three services. Female doctors were not turned away this time and served with all services – about 150 with the RAMC and a smaller number with the navy and RAF.

FANY, still a volunteer service, was still active, partly within the ATS, and formed the nucleus of motor driver companies as well as working with the Special Operations Executive (SOE), under the cover of which many courageous women trained for intelligence work behind enemy lines, including the well known names of 'Odette' and Violette Szabo.

War work and life on the Home Front

Both world wars involved civilian women to a great degree. Indeed, it seems doubtful that war could have been waged for so long if women had not stepped in to take on the jobs left vacant by men called up into

The Golden Harvest in Fields Immune from War

Gathering the harvest. An incidental duty of soldiers in training. Inset: Girl workers bringing in sheaves.

Women at work in the cornfields. Pupils who are studying farming at Colston Bassett, under the auspices of the Nottingham Education Committee. A large number of women have already shown great aptitude in farm work in the absence of men called to the Colours.

Immune from war they may have been, but these women were not immune from the effects of war. The caption writer of the War Illustrated *in 1916 records that women have 'shown great aptitude in farm work', forgetting the centuries of farm work performed by their female ancestors.*

the forces, or the behind-the-lines jobs that would free a man for fighting.

When war broke out in 1914 there was as much opposition to women taking an active role as there had been in Florence Nightingale's day. Men in industry and the trades unions that represented them had no wish to see women take on male jobs. From January 1916, however, when conscription for men was introduced for the first time, it became essential for women to fill the places left vacant, especially in the burgeoning munitions industry.

In 1915 women registered for war work and until the end of the war women took on every job that was usually performed by men. Women in your family may have worked as bus conductors, chimney sweeps or milkmen, or in factories, breweries, shipyards and coalfields (though it has to be said that finding any proof will need a great deal of luck). All classes of women were involved, and, while for middle and upper class women the war brought a new freedom and independence, for working class women life must have seemed much the same, only harder. The women who worked on munitions could sometimes be easily picked out, as exposure to TNT turned their skin yellow. They also worked with the ever-present danger from explosives; about 300 were killed by their work. Labour was needed on the land, too, as more farm labourers went off to the war and the Women's Land Service Corps was formed in 1915. Civilians also faced new dangers and hardships in that war – rationing was not introduced until 1917 and many went short of food, while the Zeppelin airships brought the war to Britain.

When the war was over, women who had worked so hard and so well were given notice. There was a feeling, particularly obvious in the press of the time, that women should get back to what they did best – keeping house and home – and let the returning soldiers take up their proper place. There was certainly little sympathy for the idea that women might want to preserve the new independence they had experienced.

The Second World War was to prove once again that women could do any job they were asked to do. In March 1941 Ernest Bevin, Minister of Labour, appealed for women to come forward to work on 'the industrial front'. By October 1942 all women aged up to 45 had been called for interview at their local Labour Exchange and any woman who refused to take up a job could face imprisonment.

However, mothers with children under 14 were not compelled to work, and there was an 'outbreak' of pregnancy in some areas! In July 1943 women aged 46–50 years were also required to register for war work. In fact, many women well over retirement age also volunteered and over half all women aged between 14 and 64 were working for the war effort, some voluntarily, by 1943. They worked in engineering, chemical and explosives works and ordnance factories, and as anything from plumbers to railway staff. Many women volunteered for the Women's Land Army (WLA); in fact, women had been registering as 'land army reserves' since 1939. The WLA was run by women and when recruiting ceased in 1943 it had nearly 90,000 women on its lists. They were poorly equipped and had to face some male opposition and very hard work, but many land girls looked back on that time with great pride and affection.

Women took on posts in civil defence, such as air raid wardens, and they joined the Women's Voluntary Service (WVS, founded 1938 and later the WRVS) to billet evacuees, run mobile canteens and pitch in whenever needed in a crisis or major incident. Nearly a million women were in the WVS by 1941. Country women particularly joined the Women's Institute (WI) and put their skills to good use by, for instance, making literally tons of jam from perishable fruits, gathering herbs, moss and rosehips for medicines and running salvage and war savings campaigns. Some women joined the Home Guard. They did all this while raising children, running a home and enduring the hardship and monotony of rationing and shortages. It should not be forgotten, too, that many women also suffered weeks or months of heavy bombing and the terrible stress of seeing friends die and familiar streets reduced to rubble around them.

Finding out more

Researching female ancestors who served with the army before the First World War will not be easy. Soldiers were not supposed to marry without the permission of their commanding officer, though many did so. The names of official army wives put 'on the strength' of the regiment in the 1800s may sometimes be recorded on **army muster rolls**.

A romantic and moving keepsake from the First World War. Written above the picture on this postcard is 'Goodbye sweetheart', and on the reverse 'night, night' and 'with much love and kisses' (17 kisses, but no names!).

This chapter is concerned with the major conflicts of the 19th and 20th centuries but army women went wherever the army went, which in Victorian times could mean anywhere in the empire. Could she have been in India at the time of the mutiny (1857), for instance, or in Afghanistan for the retreat from Kabul (1842)? *Judy O'Grady and the Colonel's Lady: The Army Wife and Camp Follower since 1660* by Noel St John Williams (Brassey's Defence Publishers, 1988) is an excellent introduction to uncovering the lives of the women who followed the army.

Writing to her soldier sweetheart: my mother writing one of her regular letters to her fiancé in 1939, with his picture on the bureau in front of her.

If your ancestor was a **nurse**, the National Archives has a useful leaflet on *Military Nurses and the Nursing Service*, which will help you find out what records may be available. If she applied to go to the Crimea with Florence Nightingale, for instance, you may find a testimonial for her. *Angels and Citizens: British Women as Military Nurses 1854–1914* by Anne Summers (Routledge & Kegan Paul, 1988) is just one book of the many that detail the campaign by Florence Nightingale and others to bring army nursing into modern times.

Tracing your First World War Ancestors by Simon Fowler (Countryside Books, 2003) has a chapter entitled 'Women and Civilians', and includes useful introductory information on nurses and the women's services. During that war, the **women's services** (except the nursing services) existed for only a short time before being demobilised as soon as hostilities were over. The National Archives' Military Records Information leaflet no. 74, *Women's Services, First World War*, will tell you what survives and is held there. Second World War **service records** are still held by the service departments and are usually only released to the person concerned or their next of kin.

One way in which you may find a reference to your ancestor is through **medal rolls** or records of **awards** made. Women may have been non-combatants, but they still performed acts of great bravery. The Queen's and King's South Africa Medals were awarded to military nurses who served in the South African War. Military nurses were also eligible for the Royal Red Cross Medal, instituted by Queen Victoria in 1883, or the Royal Red Cross 2nd Class. In 1917 the award of the Military Medal was extended to women. Individual awards will be mentioned in the *London Gazette* (search it online at *www.gazettes-online.com*) as well as being recorded in rolls at the National Archives. Servicewomen were also eligible for the same campaign medals as men – the British War Medal and Victory Medal, for instance, were awarded to all servicewomen.

There is a huge amount of information on the two world wars available in book form and on the Internet. There is space here for only a few examples: consult bibliographies for further reading and use a good search engine to seek out useful websites. The website *www.fleetairarmarchive.net/RollofHonour/Women.html*, for instance, has a tribute to the 'flying Wrens' of the Fleet Air Arm, and to ATA fliers, with a list of a few of the incidents in which the latter were involved and a memorial roll of some of the Wrens killed in action. There is a collection of material relating to the WRNS, 1917–1993, at the Royal Naval Museum, HM Naval Base (PP66), Portsmouth, Hampshire PO1 3NH, which can be viewed or used for research. The WAAF Association official website (*freespace.virgin.net/frank.haslam/waafa.html*) has a bibliography related to the WRAF/WAAF. Books which may be of help in building up background information include *Our Wartime Days: The WAAF in World War II* by Sqn Ldr B. Escott (Alan Sutton, 1995), or *The Women's Royal Army Corps* by Shelford Bidwell (Famous Regiments series; Leo Cooper, 1977).

The **Imperial War Museum** should be on your list for a visit. It has information sheets on some of the women's services; see their website (*www.iwm.org.uk*) for details of these and other publications. The Women's Work collection in the Department of Printed Books at the museum may also be worth investigating for specific research; this requires an appointment before you visit.

The Debt of Honour Register of the **Commonwealth War Graves Commission** includes details of women killed on active service during both world wars, while the Civilian Roll of Honour records 66,000 civilians killed during the Second World War. Search them easily on their website, *www.cwgc.org.uk*, or write, giving as much information about an individual as you can, to the Records and Enquiries Section, The Commonwealth War Graves Commission, 2 Marlow Road, Maidenhead, Berks SL6 7DX. (There may be a small fee for postal enquiries.)

In 1918 all women aged 30 and over were granted the parliamentary vote. This coincided with all servicemen being given the vote, no matter their age. In local county record offices you should find **absent voters' registers** for mid-1918 to 1921 and these can be extremely helpful if your ancestor was away from home with the forces, nursing or on war work. The register gives her name, home address and her current posting, whether in this country or abroad.

The 60th anniversaries of the events of the Second World War, which have been taking place since 1999, were (and still are) the spur for many local books recording experiences during that period; your local studies library or museum should be able to tell you what has been published for your area. Books such as *What did You do in the War, Mummy?* by Mavis Nicholson (Pimlico, 1996) give some idea of the scope of women's wartime experiences.

If you have never wondered how the women in your family coped with war, it's time to start thinking about it. Sadly, we can no longer ask the women who lived through the First World War, but if you have older relatives who experienced the second conflict then you should talk to them as soon as possible. Families often also have the odd bit of ephemera tucked away, such as ration books or identity cards, which will help to recreate the past, but when little primary evidence survives for individuals on the home front, personal memories are precious. You may, indeed, have lived through it yourself. If you did, make sure you write of your experiences so that future generations can have a first-hand account. (If only your female ancestors had done the same!)

A propaganda leaflet dropped by the Germans on the Allied lines in 1942, playing on the men's fears that their wives and lovers were being seduced by those 'over-sexed' American troops at home. Divorce suits did rise sharply after the war.

CHAPTER 9

Timeline 1800–1950

A selective list of some of the important facts and events that touched women's lives

1801 Women are found to outnumber men by 400,000 in the first national census.

1820 Flogging as a punishment for female offenders is abolished.

1828 Offences Against the Person Act: summary jurisdiction for common assault and battery (minor penalties) on women and children. Offence of petit treason is abolished.

1833 First Factory Act: women and children not to be employed more than 12 hours a day.

1839 Custody of Infants Act: mothers are enabled to petition the Lord Chancellor or the Master of the Rolls for an access order or, for a child under 8, a custody order.

1842 Lord Ashley's Mines Act prohibits women and children from working underground.

1847 Factory Act limits hours for women and children to no more than 10 per day.

1848 Queen's College, London is founded – for women wanting to qualify as teachers.

1851 Women's Suffrage Petition is presented to the House of Lords.

1853 Act for the Better Prevention and Punishment of Aggravated Assaults upon Women and Children: increases penalties; allows a complaint to be made by a third party.

1854 Florence Nightingale's nurses arrive in the Crimea.

1857 Divorce and Matrimonial Causes Act: *judicial divorce* – adultery only for men; wife must also prove cruelty or desertion; *judicial separation* – wife can keep what she earns; protection for deserted wives; provision to be made by the divorce court for children's custody, maintenance and education.

1864 Contagious Diseases Act (also 1866, 1869): prostitutes living in garrison towns liable to be forcibly examined for VD (act repealed 1886).

1865 Elizabeth Garrett becomes the first English-trained woman doctor to be included on the Medical Register. Women allowed to sit for Cambridge Local examinations. Dr James Barry, Inspector-General of the Army Medical Department, dies and is found to be a woman.

1867 Manchester Women's Suffrage Committee is formed by Miss Lydia Becker, soon to be followed by committees in London, Edinburgh and Bristol; National Society for Women's Suffrage is founded in London.

1869 *The Subjection of Women* by J.S. Mill is published. A College for women is founded at Hitchin, which in 1873 moved to Cambridge as Girton College. London University permits women to sit for examinations.
Municipal Franchise Act: extends the municipal vote to women ratepayers on the same terms as men.

1870 Ladies' National Association for the Repeal of the Contagious Diseases Acts is founded by Mrs Josephine Butler. Education Act: women to be allowed to serve on new School Boards. Married Women's Property Act: wages and property earned by a wife through her own work to be regarded as her separate property.

1873 Infant Custody Act: age of children whose custody could be granted to the mother is raised to 16; the exception of mothers found guilty of adultery is abolished.

1874 Women's Protective and Provident League is founded (later Women's Trade Union League).

1876 Act is passed requiring all medical licensing bodies in Great Britain to open their examinations to women, but at their discretion.

1878 Matrimonial Causes Act: JPs and judges are given the power to grant judicial separation to a wife whose husband has been convicted of aggravated assault upon her, plus the custody of her children under 10 and weekly maintenance.

1881 Army Nursing Service is formed.

1882 Married Women's Property Act: principle of 1870 is extended to all property, regardless of the source or when acquired. A wife now has a statutorily separate estate, with her own rights and duties; she can dispose of it in her lifetime or bequeath it in her will; she can enter into contracts, sue and be sued (she could even sue her husband, or prosecute him if he were to steal her property).

1884 Matrimonial Causes Act: removes imprisonment for contempt if a woman fails to comply with a decree for restitution of conjugal rights; if a husband refuses to return to his wife he can be ordered by a court to make her an allowance; if a wife runs off, the court can order a settlement of her separate property for the benefit of husband and children; if she has her own business or earnings, she may be ordered to make an allowance. (Known as 'Mrs Weldon's Act', after a woman who had tried to force her husband to return to live with her and restore her conjugal rights, the Matrimonial Causes Act shows that judges were now conceding that they could not force people to live together.)

1886 Guardianship of Infants Act permits a mother to apply to the Chancery Division of the High Court, or the county court for custody of or access to her child/children – no age limit on the child; and a surviving mother to have joint-guardianship, even if the deceased father or court had appointed a guardian.

1888 Bryant & May matchgirls strike.

1889 Lady Sandhurst is elected to London County Council; she is not allowed to take her seat.

1892 Quarter of a million sign a petition to Parliament for votes for women.

1895 Summary Jurisdiction (Married Women) Act: extends the 1878 act, granting separation orders if deserted by the husband, or forced by wilful neglect or persistent cruelty to leave him, or if he has been sentenced for assaulting her; custody of children under 16; and weekly maintenance of up to £2.

1897 National Union of Women's Suffrage Societies is founded (president, Mrs Millicent Fawcett) with about 500 affiliated societies.

1900 Charlotte Cooper becomes first British woman Olympic gold medallist (tennis).

1903 Tribunal of judges refuses to admit Miss Bertha Cave to the Bar on the grounds that there is no precedent for female lawyers.

Women's Social and Political Union founded by Mrs Pankhurst at Manchester.

1904 Ladies' Automobile Club holds its first meeting. Marie Stopes is appointed first female science lecturer at Manchester.

1905 First disruption of a political meeting, Manchester, by suffragettes; Christabel Pankhurst and Annie Kenney imprisoned.

1906 First cross-Channel flight by a woman – Mrs Griffith Brewer – in a balloon. Mrs Emmeline Pethwick-Lawrence becomes treasurer of the Women's Social and Political Union.

Daily Mail coins the word 'suffragettes'; Theresa Billington becomes the first suffragette to be sent to Holloway Prison.

National Federation of Women Workers is formed.

1907 Qualification of Women Act enables women to sit as councillors, aldermen, mayors, or chairmen on county or borough councils. Marriage to Deceased Wife's Sister Act. Women's Freedom League formed.

1908 First woman mayor in UK is elected (Dr Elizabeth Garrett-Anderson) at Aldeburgh, Suffolk. Miss Edith New is first suffragette to chain herself to railings outside 10 Downing Street.

1909 First aerial leaflet raid carried out on London by suffragette Muriel Matters, by airship; Miss Marion Wallace-Dunlop is the first suffragette hunger-striker; force-feeding begins.

1910 First two women members of London County Council elected. Girl Guides formed.

1911 Boycott of census by suffragette sympathisers.

1912 First aeroplane Channel flight by a woman, Harriet Quimby: Deal to Cap Gris Nez.

1913 'Cat and Mouse' Act enables authorities to free hunger-striking suffragettes from prison if they look like dying and re-arrest when they are well again. Death of Miss Emily Davison at Ascot races; suffragette campaign escalates into arson and bomb attacks. Constitutionalist suffragists hold a peaceful pilgrimage to London, women coming from all over the country. Miss Emily Duncan is appointed first woman magistrate, West Ham.

1915 Women's Land Service Corps is formed. Register of women for war service.

1916 Royal College of Nursing is founded.

1917 Women's Army Auxiliary Corps is founded (WAAC; renamed Queen Mary's AAC in 1918). Women's Royal Naval Service (WRNS) is founded.

1918 Royal Air Force Nursing Service is formed. Women's Royal Air Force (WRAF) is formed. Electoral Reform Act: vote is granted to women aged 30 and over (6 million women); also the Parliament (Qualification of Women) Act allows women to stand for Parliament. Marie Stopes publishes *Married Love*; the references to contraception cause controversy.

1919 First parliamentary election at which women can vote; at a by-election Mrs Nancy Astor is elected first woman Member of Parliament.
Sex Disqualification Removal Act: women may not be excluded because of their sex from public office or the professions.

1920 Women admitted to full membership at Oxford University.

1921 National registration for civilian nurses established. First women sit on a divorce court jury.

1922 Infanticide, the killing of a new-born baby by its mother, becomes a statutory offence.

1923 Legitimacy Act: parents enabled to legitimise a child by marrying after its birth. Matrimonial Causes Act: wives enabled to divorce husbands solely for adultery.

1928 Women granted equal franchise with men, all at age 21.

1929 Women voters outnumber the men in the general election. Margaret Bondfield, Labour MP for Northampton, becomes the first woman privy councillor and cabinet minister.

1930 Amy Johnson is the first woman to fly solo to Australia.

1936 BBC appoints its first women announcers: Jasmine Bligh and Elizabeth Cowell.

1937 Marriage Act reforms divorce laws: no divorce allowed in the first three years of marriage.

1938 Women's Voluntary Service (later WRVS) is formed. Auxiliary Territorial Service (ATS) formed.

1939 Women's Royal Naval Service (WRNS) re-formed. Women's Auxiliary Air Force (WAAF) formed. Recruitment for Women's Land Army begins.

1940 Air Transport Auxiliary admits women pilots and ground crew.

1941 National Service Act: compulsory call-up for military service or police/fire services for single women and childless widows (19–30). Registration of women for war work on the industrial front. First Wrens are sent overseas.

1942 First mixed searchlight regiment is formed.

1943 Part-time war work is made compulsory for women aged 18–45; those aged 46–50 required to register.

1946 Transit camp is set up for the c.50,000 GI brides on their way to America. Women are admitted to appointment in the diplomatic service (but marriage bar operates). Divorce: decree absolute to follow six weeks after decree nisi, not six months.

1947 Birthrate is the highest for 26 years.

1948 Women's Service Act: ATS becomes the Women's Royal Army Corps and the WAAF becomes the Women's Royal Air Force, incorporated into the armed forces in 1949. Women admitted to full membership at Cambridge University.

Appendix
A word about sources

It is unfortunately not possible in a book of this length to go into explanations about records and archives in depth. Please read a good guide to tracing family history for more information on many of the general genealogical subjects touched on (substituting 'she' for 'he'!) such as census returns, wills, newspapers, military and occupational sources and so on: *Ancestral Trails* by Mark Herber (Sutton Publishing, 1997), *Tracing your Family Tree* by Jean Cole and John Titford (Countryside Books, 1997, 4th edition 2003), or *Explore your Family's Past* (Reader's Digest, 2000), for instance. The annual edition of *The Family and Local History Handbook* (Genealogical Services Directory, 7th edition, 2003) is extremely useful for up-to-date information on addresses and websites. *Tracing your Ancestors in the Public Record Office* by Amanda Bevan (PRO, 6th edition, 2002) introduces the sources in the National Archives, and there are other more specialist books in their catalogue. Family history magazines include *Family Tree Magazine*, *Family History Monthly* and *Ancestors* (the latter only available by subscription from the National Archives).

Addresses for archives and societies not already given in the text:
The National Archives (Public Record Office), Ruskin Avenue, Kew, Richmond TW9 4DU
Telephone: 020 8876 3444; website: *www.nationalarchives.gov.uk*

Family Records Centre, 1 Myddleton Street, London EC1R 1UW
Telephone: 020 8392 5300; website: *www.familyrecords.gov.uk*

British Library Newspaper Library, Colindale Avenue, London NW9 5HE
Telephone: 020 7412 7353; website: *www.bl.uk/collections/newspaper*

Principal Probate Registry, First Avenue House, 42–49 High Holborn, London WC1
Telephone: 020 7947 6939; website: *www.courtservice.gov.uk*

Society of Genealogists, 14 Charterhouse Buildings, Goswell Road, London EC1M 7BA
Telephone: 020 7251 8799; website: *www.sog.org.uk*

Imperial War Museum, Lambeth Road, London SE1 6HZ
Telephone: 020 7416 5348; website: *www.iwm.org.uk*

Federation of Family History Societies, PO Box 2425, Coventry CV5 6YX
Telephone: 070 4149 2032; website: *www.ffhs.org.uk/General/Members/index.htm*

Acknowledgements

My thanks to Terry Pankhurst and to my other friends who offered their precious family photographs; to the staff at Hertfordshire Archives & Local Studies, St Albans Library and the Central Resources Library, Hatfield; and to Jean Cole for her helpful comments and advice, as well as to Nicholas Battle and Paula Leigh at Countryside Books who have given me so much encouragement. Much of the background reading and research behind this book has built up gradually over the years; as a family historian, I am of course indebted to the staff at the National Archives, the Family Records Centre, the Imperial War Museum, the British Library Newspaper Library and the other repositories mentioned in this book.

Bibliography

The books mentioned in the text are listed below for easy reference, with the addition of a number of other books that I have come across and which may be of interest.

Adams, Carol, *Ordinary Lives a Hundred Years Ago*, Virago Press, 1982

Beeton, Isabella, *Book of Household Management* [1859–61], facs 1st edn Chancellor Press, 1982

Bidwell, Shelford, *The Women's Royal Army Corps*, Leo Cooper, 1977

Bourne, S., & Chicken, A.H., *Records of the Medical Profession*, Bourne & Chicken, 1994

Brittain, Vera, *Testament of Youth*, Virago Press, 1992

Burnett, John (ed), *Destiny Obscure: Autobiographies of Childhood, Education and Family from the 1820s to the 1920s*, Allen Lane, 1982

Chapman, Colin, *Ecclesiastical Courts: Their Officials and their Records*, Lochin Publishing, 1992

Chapman, Colin, *Marriage Laws, Rites, Records and Customs*, Lochin Publishing, 1997

Crawford, Elizabeth, *The Women's Suffrage Movement: A Reference Guide 1866–1928*, Routledge Kegan Paul, 2000
Crow, Duncan, *The Victorian Woman*, National Book Network, 1972
Crow, Duncan, *The Edwardian Woman*, Allen & Unwin, 1978
Cunnington, Phillis & Lucas, Catherine, *Charity Costumes*, A & C Black, 1978
Cunnington, Phillis & Lucas, Catherine, *Costume for Births, Marriages and Deaths*, A & C Black, 1972
Cunnington, Phillis & Lucas, Catherine, *Occupational Costume in England*, A & C Black, 1968
Davidson, Caroline, *A Woman's Work is Never Done: A History of Housework in the British Isles 1650–1900*, Chatto & Windus, 1986
Dawes, Frank, *Not in Front of the Servants*, Random Century, 1989
Dudgeon, Piers (ed), *Village Voices: A Portrait of Change in England's Green and Pleasant Land 1915–1990*, WI Books Ltd, 1989
Escott, B., *Our Wartime Days: The WAAF in World War Two*, Alan Sutton, 1995
Ewing, Elizabeth, *Everyday Dress 1650–1900*, Batsford, 1984
Fisher, Trevor, *Prostitution and the Victorians*, Pimlico, 1999
Ford, Colin (ed), *The Story of Popular Photography*, National Museum of Photography, Film & Television, 1989
Fowler, Simon, *Tracing Your First World War Ancestors*, Countryside Books, 2003
Fraser, Flora, *The English Gentlewoman*, Barrie & Jenkins, 1987
Fussell, G.E. & K.R., *The English Countrywoman*, Orbis, 1981
Hawkings, David, *Bound for Australia*, Phillimore, 1987
Hawkings, David, *Criminal Ancestors*, Sutton, rev edn 1996
Hay, Ian, *One Hundred Years of Army Nursing*, Cassel & Co, 1952
Hiley, Michael, *Victorian Working Women: Portraits from Life*, Gordon Fraser Gallery, 1979
Hill, Bridget, *Women Alone: Spinsters in England 1650–1850*, Yale University Press, 2001
Holcombe, Lee, *Wives and Property: Reform of the Married Woman's Property Law in Nineteenth Century England*, University of Toronto Press, 1983
Holdsworth, Angela, *Out of the Doll's House*, BBC Books, 1988
Horn, Pamela, *Labouring Life in the Victorian Countryside*, Alan Sutton, 1987
Horn, Pamela, *The Rise and Fall of the Victorian Servant*, Alan Sutton, 1995
Horn, Pamela, *The Victorian and Edwardian Schoolchild*, Alan Sutton, 1989
Hughes, Kathryn, *The Victorian Governess*, Hambleden Press, 1993
John, Angela V., *Coalmining Women*, Cambridge University Press, 1984
Lansdell, Avril, *Fashion a la carte 1860–1900*, Shire, 1985

Liddington, Jill & Norris, Jill, *One Hand Tied Behind Us: The Rise of the Women's Suffrage Movement*, Rivers Oram, 2000
Lummis, Trevor & Marsh, Jan, *The Woman's Domain: Women and the English Country House*, Penguin, 1993
Macdonald, Lyn, *The Roses of No Man's Land*, Penguin, 1993
Marlow, Joyce (ed), *The Virago Book of Women and the Great War*, Virago Press, 1999
May, Trevor, *The Victorian Domestic Servant*, Shire, 2001
Mingay, G.E., *Rural Life in Victorian England*, Sutton Publishing, 1998
Nicholson, Mavis, *What Did You Do In the War, Mummy?*, Pimlico, 1996
Pember Reeves, Maud, *Round About a Pound a Week,* [1913] Virago, 1999
Piggott, Juliet, *Queen Alexandra's Royal Army Nursing Corps*, Leo Cooper, 1975
Pols, Robert, *Dating Old Photographs*, FFHS, 2nd ed 1998
Pols, Robert, *Family Photographs 1860–1945*, PRO, 2002
Pols, Robert, *Looking at Old Photographs; Their Dating and Interpretation*, FFHS, 1999
Popham, Hugh, *FANY: The Story of the Women's Transport Service 1907–1984,* Leo Cooper, 1984
Powell, Bob & Westacott, Nigel, *The Women's Land Army 1939–1950*, Sutton Publishing, 1997
Priestley, Philip, *Victorian Prison Lives*, Pimlico, 1999
Rees, Sian, *The Floating Brothel*, Headline, 2001
Roberts, Robert, *The Classic Slum: Salford Life in the First Quarter of the Century*, Pelican, 1973
Roberts, Robert, *A Ragged Schooling*, Fontana 1984
Robinson, Jane, *Wayward Women: A Guide to Women Travellers*, Oxford University Press, 1991
St John Williams, Noel, *Judy O'Grady and the Colonel's Lady: The Army Wife and Camp Follower Since 1660*, Brassey's Defence Publishers, 1988
Stone, Lawrence, *Road to Divorce; England 1530–1987*, Oxford University Press, 1995
Summers, Anne, *Angels and Citizens: British Women as Military Nurses 1854–1919*, Routledge & Kegan Paul, 1988
Sykes, Brian, *The Seven Daughters of Eve*, Corgi, 2002
Thompson, F.M.L. *The Rise of Respectable Society: A Social History of Victorian Britain 1830–1900*, Fontana 1988
Thompson, Flora, *Lark Rise to Candleford*, [1945] Penguin, 2000
Trollope, Joanna, *Britannia's Daughters: Women of the British Empire*, Random House, 1983
Wadge, Collett, *Women in Uniform*, Sampson Low, Marston & Co, 1946
W.I., *Within Living Memory* county series, Countryside Books

Index